The TAO *of* TAYLOR SWIFT

LINDSEY SMITH

The TAO *of* TAYLOR SWIFT

13 PRINCIPLES TO LIVE A HAPPY, FREE, AND BALANCED LIFE

weldonowen

Contents

Introduction

When I was twelve years old, I had a debilitating panic attack that left me hospitalized.

Desperate for solutions, my family was committed to trying any method that might help me. In my small rural Pennsylvania town there just happened to be a wellness center that helped people with anxiety through mindfulness, and my parents signed me up immediately.

I started seeing a qigong expert, Dr. Ted. We started practicing breathing exercises, I learned tai chi, and most importantly, he listened to me share my feelings and encouraged me to journal. It was also the first time I was introduced to Taoism. Within a year of seeing him, I went from someone who had panic attacks every day at school to someone who wrote a tiny book called *Maxin' and Relaxin'*, teaching other students how to reduce stress in their life. I even gave presentations on it at schools throughout the state of Pennsylvania.

Then in 2006, as I was in my senior year of high school, I discovered a new spiritual teacher, one who would be there for me through life events like homecoming and prom, college graduation, buying my first house, adopting my dog, and getting married. That other spiritual teacher is Ms. Taylor Alison Swift.

Her teachings started with her words. She was raw and honest with her feelings, naming names, and being unapologetically herself. I was inspired. Could I use my voice in big ways in my life? Could I share my feelings more and more with the world?

Eventually, I started following her on MySpace and Instagram, and I devoured every magazine article, watched every interview, and soaked up every ounce of wisdom I could glean from her. I was amazed at her openness, her connection to her fans, and her playfulness. I remember discovering the Easter egg liner notes in real time with other Swifties and feeling like I was a part of something for the first time.

I then watched her get criticized and scrutinized and called out and bullied on a public stage and how she handled it by continuing to make art and showing up as her authentic self. At my darkest times with loss of friendships and business relationships, her courage inspired me. Could I be courageous? Could I continue to adapt and grow?

And then I got to experience Taylor through her stadium tours and sold-out shows. I got to see the absolute joy she radiated on stage. The dedication to her craft. The gratitude she had for everyone on that stage and in the audience. This woman was going after her dreams and making it. How can I show up to my dreams in big ways?

In examining my connection with Taylor over the years, I realized her teachings are very similar to the Tao teachings I learned as a kid.

The Tao is understood as the general life force that flows through everything in the universe. The Tao cannot be described with words but must be experienced and lived.

Similarly, it's one thing to listen to the words of Taylor Swift, but it's a whole otherworldly experience to witness her live. To see her interact with fans. To watch her in interviews. To see her adapt to scrutiny and heartache. To see her accept her multitudes.

Long story short: Taylor's art and life mirror many of the principles of Taoism.

Combining these two sources of wisdom has allowed me to harness both the spirit of Tao and the power of Taylor to live a happy, free, and balanced life, mostly at the same time.

The Tao and Taylor

There is one thing that is certain: the Tao Te Ching *is a prized work of spiritual and philosophical text. At only five-thousand-ish words, it packs a big punch, and it's no wonder this text has stood the test of time. In fact, I find myself rereading it or exploring new translations, and every time I go back to it, it's like I see something new for the first time. This especially rings true depending on where I am in my life and what I am going through.*

I think that is the thing with words and art—from a spiritual text like the *Tao Te Ching* to lyrics from a pop star like Taylor Swift. We can listen to or read something over and over again, but depending on where we are in life, it gives us new meaning, new inspiration, new hope, or even a sense of joy or peace.

In fact, when the *Red* album launched, the song "All Too Well" hit me at a time when I was experiencing an intense breakup. I remember driving around screaming the song inside my car as a cathartic release. However, when "All Too Well (10-Minute Version)" launched nearly nine years later, I was in a much happier spot and experiencing this song transformed into screaming it with pure joy alongside tens of thousands of other fans at The Eras Tour.

When *evermore* launched, I was grieving the fallout of a business relationship, and the song "closure" was especially pivotal in processing those feelings. The song "happiness" was my go-to anthem that got me through my late-in-life ADHD diagnosis. However, when I listen to those songs now, on the other side of healing, I appreciate them in different ways.

Similar to the *Tao*. When I read it as a preteen and young adult, I was struggling with finding my way in this world and dealing with debilitating anxiety. The *Tao* was there to remind me to go with the flow of the universe and to help bring more compassion to myself and others. Now, rereading as an adult, I'm finding such power in the yin and yang and the dualities that exist in the world and (attempting) to cultivate a deep sense of trust that all will balance out naturally and that the world is not black and white, but instead, full of beautiful duality, or screaming color.

In the foreword for the *1989* album, Taylor wrote, "These songs were once about my life. They are now about yours." Like the songs of Taylor, the *Tao* doesn't have or claim ownership on the text, instead, it becomes what you need. That's the thing about art and philosophy—they take on meaning to the person listening or reading. I doubt Taylor Swift wrote the song "happiness" thinking that it was going to be an ADHD anthem for little old me. In fact, I absolutely know that was not a thought of hers at all. Why would it be? Similarly, I doubt Lao-tzu could even dream of a world in which his text connected with the masses years later, considering all the advances and changes in the world (although there is a reason why it is ancient wisdom!). And I highly doubt either of them thought of a world in which connecting pop culture with ancient wisdom could or would be done. But that is the thing about art and creation and continuing to go with the flow where life takes you—oftentimes, it shows you the way.

Ultimately, this book comes from my own space of reflection. In fact, writing this book came at a time when I needed it the most. With so much turmoil in the world, I found myself coming back again to these two forms of wisdom—Taylor and the Tao. I put them both on like an old cardigan, and they gave me the comfort and support when I needed it most. Now, it is my hope, Dear Reader, that you will take these stories and make them your own.

SECTION ONE

Life Is Like a Willow

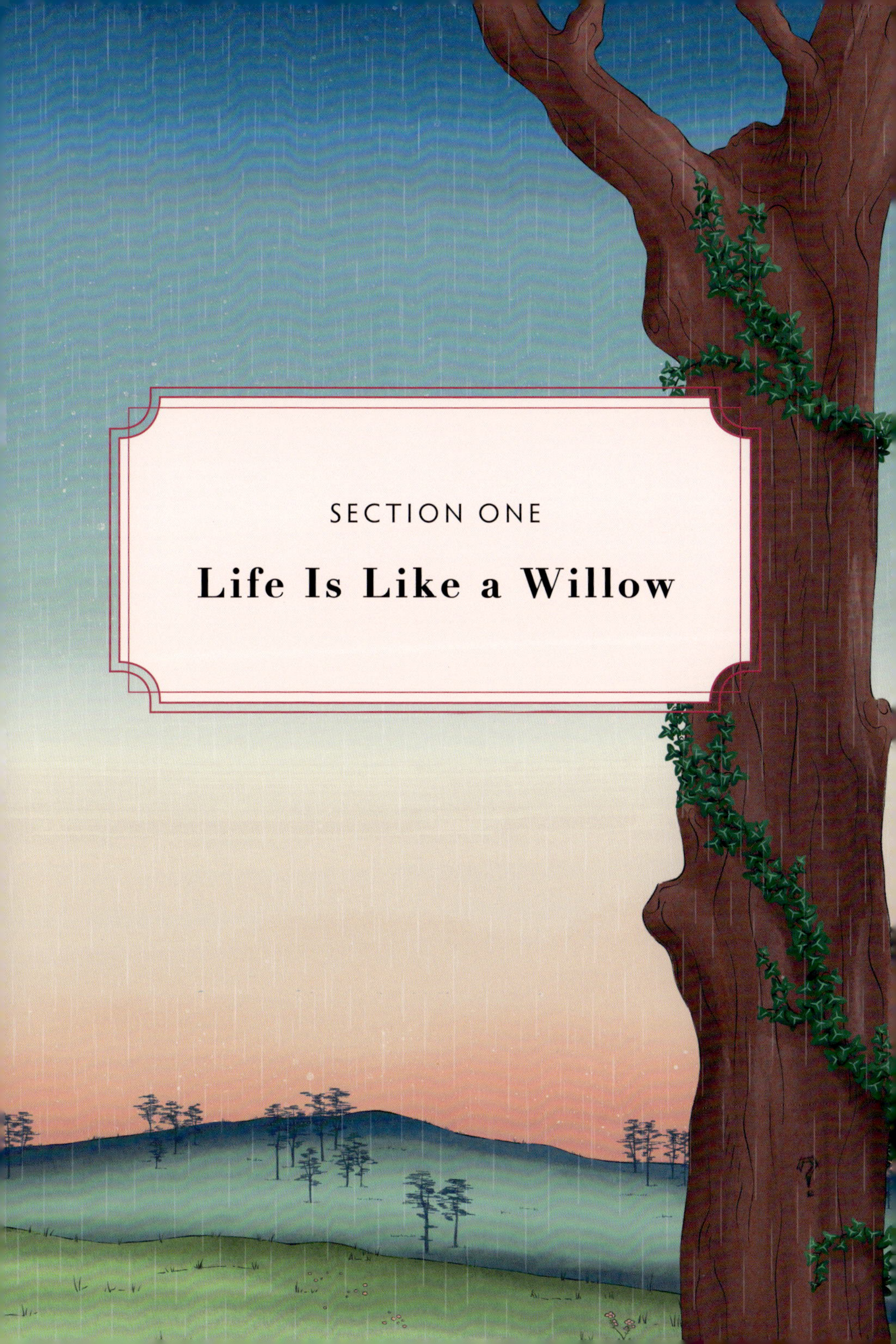

The best leaders value their words and use them sparingly.

THE *TAO*, CHAPTER 17

There will be no further explanation. There will just be reputation.

TAYLOR

Describing the Tao, in many ways, is an impossible feat. The Tao itself says that it cannot be explained because it is eternal. The Tao is simply the Way, and using words to try to describe it is not enough as there is nothing as powerful to the mind or spirit to do it justice. The Tao cannot often be described by words; instead, it must be experienced and lived. Explanations do not do it justice.

However, in its basic essence, the Tao is understood as the general life force that everything in the universe flows through, or forever going with the flow. In the Tao, everything has its place and that's part of the natural flow of our existence. By being in flow with the natural cycles of the universe, we can learn, adapt, and work with anything that comes our way, just as the changing seasons teach us. True happiness comes from embracing all the damn seasons and changes, not fighting against them.

I think it's easiest to start noticing this when you can take a bird's-eye view of your life. In moments of despair or heartache or sadness, it's easy to sit and dwell in those feelings. It's easy to think things like, "Why did this happen to me?" or "What did I do to deserve this?" It's a lot harder to sit with those emotions and feelings in the moment, knowing that they are just a part of your bigger journey.

For someone like Taylor Swift, her life has been public since she was a teenager. We've seen her go from a wide-eyed country singer to a full-blown pop star in less than two decades. In all of the ups and downs, we have watched this play out in her own life and how she continues to shake it off and go with the flow of where life is taking her. Yes, she is a detailed planner, but there have been so many things she has been forced to confront publicly and no matter what, she keeps going on her path.

During the *Reputation* era, Taylor said, "There will be no further explanation. There will just be reputation." Much like the Tao, that album could not be explained, it could only be shared, experienced, and lived. And now, there will be no formal explanation, there will just be *The Tao of Taylor Swift*.

MEDITATION 1

Meet Me in the Pouring Rain

In 2011, Taylor played one of her rainiest rain shows ever at Gillette Stadium in Foxborough, Massachusetts, on her Speak Now World Tour.

Leading up to the concert, she was so worried about the rain and how it would impact the show. She couldn't help but wonder: Would people even show up? Would the stadium be empty? Should she cancel?

However, it was still safe to perform and as a person of her word, Taylor decided to continue the concert with no edits.

As soon as she appeared on stage in her sequined gold dress and sang the first line of "Sparks Fly," the crowd, drenched from head to toe, went wild. She continued to perform the full eighteen-song set in the rain with her dancers, band, and stage props. This went down as one of those magical moments in fan history. She was filled with nothing but wonder and amazement that the fans stayed and she embraced this moment

THIS IS ME TRYING

Next time you experience something out of your control, meet it in the pouring rain. You might get soaked, but might also have the time of your life.

they were all experiencing together. It became one of the most beloved tour moments in Taylor's tour history and a reason why she loves rain shows to this day. She makes the best of a rainy situation and because of that, her fans have the time of their lives dancing in the rain with her.

Similar to how Taylor responded to the rain show, Taoism is also about forever going with the flow of the universe. In life, there are so many things that are out of our control—whether it's a rainstorm during an important event, coming down with an illness when on vacation, or being laid off from your job.

When it rains in your life, how can you make the best of the experience and stay present the best you can? If you're laid off from your job, maybe this is a time to explore new interests and hobbies. You might just find the next best career. If you come down with an illness on vacation, maybe it's a reminder to slow down in your day-to-day life.

MEDITATION 2

Act Swiftly and Subtly

One of my favorite parts about the Internet during The Eras Tour was being able to watch grainy livestream videos of the complete set—including fun countdowns of the highly anticipated surprise songs. I also loved seeing clips that fans lovingly dubbed "The Errors Tour," which were usually anything from Taylor's wardrobe issues to lyric slips to stage malfunctions. For fans, these moments became part of the magic of a live show—and a great reminder that yes, even Taylor makes mistakes.

When met with an error on stage, Taylor acts swiftly, subtly, and even playfully. When the stage malfunctioned and didn't drop her under the stage to prepare for the next set, Taylor ran full speed ahead to get out of the doors in order to continue with the timing. She later commented on a fan video that caught the infamous moment and said, "still swift af boi." During the infamous "22 hat" set where she gives an audience member a special hat during the song performance of "22," she accidentally invited the child onto the stage and quickly realized that was not right. Later in the show, she commented that her excitement and the cuteness of the young child caused her to accidentally invite her on stage.

The *Tao* shares that great leaders act subtly and often adapt rather than force outcomes. We see this perfectly in how Taylor swiftly adapted to the stage errors while also being playful about it later, showing that she adapts to stressful moments with ease.

When Taylor later released *The Eras Tour* movie, she made sure to include a special bloopers reel at the end, with many of the fan favorite "errors tour" videos shared online. While she could have created a completely polished version, this shows that she not only brought the realness that is a live show to the movie, but it also shows that she's able to shake it off and continue.

THIS IS ME TRYING

What are times when you adapted to a situation rather than forced it? How were the outcomes different? And what did you learn along the way?

MEDITATION 3

Bend When You Can

Taylor has written songs both with collaborators and by herself. She starred in her music videos and directed a short film. She's recorded songs in a professional studio and in her bedroom during COVID-19. She's written lyrics in her journals with quill ink, a fountain pen, and glitter gel ink.

Before the pandemic, Taylor was planning on releasing a next single from her *Lover* album and was gearing up for Lover Fest, which was a series of select live shows to celebrate the album. However, the lockdown canceled all her plans with no hope of getting a call that it would be over soon and she could go back to normal.

THIS IS ME TRYING

If you find yourself at a place of change of direction, get curious on how you can bend with the situation rather than let it break you.

When that happened, Taylor didn't resist or push back, but she instead continued to go with the flow and that led her to create two albums, *folklore* and *evermore*. When announcing *folklore* in July 2020, she took to social media to share this unexpected launch and said, "Before this year I probably would've overthought when to release this music at the 'perfect' time, but the times we're living in keep reminding me that nothing is guaranteed. My gut is telling me that if you make something you love, you should just put it out into the world. That's the side of uncertainty I can get on board with."

Long story short: Taylor isn't afraid to bend or adapt when she needs to. One of the main principles of the Tao is having flexibility and being able to bend like the green grass found in Centennial Park, flow like a willow tree, or ripple on like the water does at the lakes. Having peace and harmony in life comes from the willingness to change direction, no matter what comes your way.

MEDITATION 4

Embrace the Damn Seasons

Across all of Taylor's albums, she uses themes of nature as metaphors to capture her feelings and to set the scene for the time and place.

In the song "Forever Winter," she uses the opposing seasons of summer and winter to paint a picture of how it will feel if you stay in the relationship (aka summer) or if you go (aka winter). In the song "ME!," she then uses winter and summer as a reference to if you are down and out (winter), then I can be your happiness (summer). She also sets scenes in autumn and spring, using the season to evoke emotions of time and place. She has songs referencing other parts of nature like her songs called "ivy" and "the lakes."

In the *Tao Te Ching*, nature is also used throughout the text as a beautiful living metaphor for how the universe works. Each season can teach us something and naturally fills us with what we need as we continue to the next season. Every lesson we learn about life, love, leadership, and change can be reflected by what we observe in the world around us. Nature in and of itself is a teacher, and we see that both in Taylor's work and the *Tao*.

By tuning in to the seasons and elements nature shows us, we can use that to see reflections of our own life's seasonal cycles. Some seasons might be dedicated to something specific (like, maybe a tour or an album release) and others might be a slower, more intentional season (like resting and reflecting).

Nature can also put things into perspective for us. For example, if we didn't experience the cold, how would we know what it's like to feel warm? If the leaves didn't die in the winter, how could spring break loose and grow back so beautiful?

THIS IS ME TRYING

What can we learn from nature's existence that we can use in our own life? What experiences and perspectives do the actual seasons or your life seasons give that you can take as you continue along your path?

MEDITATION 5

Choose a Path

Taylor has been very clear about some of the tradeoffs she has made because of her career choice that puts her in the public spotlight. For example, she can no longer walk down the street, as she gets bombarded by people at all angles. She has security with her at all times to protect her safety. From the time she steps outside her house, cameras and strangers with cell phones capture her every move. In her documentary, Miss Americana, *we learned that her dad even had to buy her armored vehicles for an added layer of protection when traveling by car. At the least, she is missing out on going grocery shopping, but at the worst, it can feel scary and overwhelming.*

THIS IS ME TRYING

Reflect on your own career or life path. Are you hoping and wishing for a path with no challenges or are you instead allowing yourself to walk fully along the path that you've chosen? Can you release the need to want everything at once right now and instead trust the path ahead?

However, in an *NME* interview, Taylor was asked if she thought about the things she lost or had to give up as a result of her music career. In the simplest term, she said no. She elaborated, "There's no way to travel two roads at once. You pick one. And if you don't like the road you're on, you change direction. You don't sit there and go, 'Oh, I wish I could have all the good things in the world and none of the bad things.' It doesn't work like that."

To walk in harmony with the Tao, it's finding acceptance in the whole journey, just as Taylor is articulating. She is demonstrating that there are no real absolutes in your life's journey, but instead, you choose a path most authentic to you and try to move through that path with as much ease and natural flow as you can. If you find yourself resisting or not liking it, change course so you can ride the waves with more ease. Taylor recognizes the dualities that exist within her career and how both "good" and "bad" are not separate from her, but essentially a part of the same.

MEDITATION 6

It's a State of Grace

The world seems to be at a boiling point. Climate disasters, mass shootings, war, and disease. We are constantly being bombarded by alarming news cycles, and unprecedented event after unprecedented event. This is a lot for both the mind and the body to take on. To add fuel to the fire, most of this now is seen and available at our fingertips through social media and our smartphones. With opinions, videos, and new stories coming in at every angle, the noise can become too much and we can be left wondering if we will ever have peace again.

THIS IS ME TRYING

When the world erupts one way, can you resist the urge to add fuel to the fire and instead take time to sit in stillness? Can you trust that even in the chaos, the Tao is working toward harmony and balance? This doesn't mean that you cannot stand up for what is right and just, but can you ground yourself first? And most important, can you find a state of grace within yourself? That sense of peace is waiting for you in the silence.

In Taylor's song "Miss Americana & the Heartbreak Prince," Taylor reflects on all the turmoil and chaos happening in the world, sharing how she is scared, upset, and feeling helpless, wondering how we might ever overcome this.

Meeting violence with violence is not the Way of the Tao. Weapons are only used as instruments of fear, whereas in the Tao, peace and tranquility are valued above all. While it can be hard to imagine peace when violence seems to be all around, the Tao reminds us that violence we are seeing will eventually create seeds for peace and the imbalance carries within it the path to balance.

The Tao reminds us that we cannot control outward turmoil around us, but we can turn inward to find stillness. While that cannot change what is happening, it can help us find tiny pockets of peace to continue forward. By remaining inwardly still and rooted, we can better handle the storms ahead rather than getting washed away by them.

SECTION TWO

Oh So Effortless!

Mastery of the world is achieved by letting things take their natural course. You cannot master the world by changing the natural way.

THE *TAO*, CHAPTER 48

It took a while to understand the beauty of just letting go.

TAYLOR

In Taoism, there is a concept called wu wei. *(Pronounced "woo way"—or, as my brain likes to think of it, "wuuuu wheEeEeE" in Taylor language.) It essentially means effortless action or non-doing. However, it doesn't mean that you do nothing and hope for the best. It also doesn't mean that that work itself isn't challenging. Instead, it means that you don't try to force things to happen and instead, soften to trust that the timing is just right. Like Taylor, she works super hard, but she works with the flow. By embracing the "wu wei" spirit, she makes playing the guitar and performing seem oh so effortless.*

In work, this can look like letting go of a project or changing direction altogether. Maybe the timing wasn't right, or maybe you need to learn a new skill before tackling it. In relationships, this can look like meeting someone where they are rather than immediately jumping to conclusions. And when it comes to creativity, it can look like not putting pressure on yourself to come up with "the next best thing" and instead allowing yourself space to write, doodle, draw, and create for fun—as oftentimes the best ideas come when they are not forced.

During the preparation for The Eras Tour, Taylor discussed her rigorous routine and how she rehearsed for the three-and-a-half-hour show. She started preparing her body months in advance by singing the set while running at the pacing of that set on the treadmill, she quit drinking alcohol, and she focused on getting her mind and body aligned. When it came to actually rehearsing the set, she said she was able to run the show in the stadium for almost a month before the first show, saying, "I wanted to get it in my bones. I wanted to be so over-rehearsed that I could be silly with the fans and not lose my train of thought."

The work she put in ultimately paid off. She could perform the three-and-a-half-hour set with ease and bring her playfulness to various parts of the set rather than it being a rigorous act.

Similarly, when Taylor first started playing guitar as a young teenage girl, she would practice for hours and hours, so much that her fingers would bleed. When you know something so deeply and put in the advance work to align your mind and body, it's easier to act without strain.

MEDITATION 1

Genres Don't Define Her

One of the core teachings of the Tao is that it cannot be defined. To define it limits it and the Tao is limitless. The Tao is a great metaphor for how human beings exist and operate in the world. We often like to put ourselves in boxes and define everything. Boxing ourselves in can often cloud creativity, preventing us from exploring our curiosities and wonders. At worst, it can prevent true innovation from happening because we try to fit within the limitations already set. Our true nature, however, contains multitudes and cannot be singularly defined. As soon as we try to label or define something, we suddenly reduce its wholeness to a narrow slice.

THIS IS ME TRYING

Think about labels you might have put on yourself or others. What labels do you hold on to tightly and how might releasing them allow you to live more fully in the flow?

From early on, Taylor did not want to be defined or boxed in creatively by genres. In fact, she has consistently mentioned how she likes to change things up and try different things when it comes to her music. We see this as she has experimented with country, pop, rock, folk, and others.

After *Red* launched, Taylor was asked if she was still a country artist since this new album contained several pop-sounding crossover songs, or what Taylor would later refer to as "a real patchwork of genres." Her response: "I leave the genre labeling to other people. I really do. If I were to think too hard about it, that would stifle you creatively. If you think too hard about who other people want you to be as an artist, it stops you from being who you want to be as an artist."

Like the Tao, it can't be defined by one thing, and neither should we. Like Taylor said, "For me, genres are a way for people to easily categorize music. But it doesn't have to define you. It doesn't have to limit you."

MEDITATION 2

It All Makes Sense

Taylor's album Red *took the charts by storm with her hits like "22" and "We Are Never Ever Getting Back Together." However, when it came to music industry critics, most said that the album teetered the line of country and pop and didn't have one cohesive sound.*

When she was up for Grammy of the Year Award in 2013 for the *Red* album, she lost. While she admitted the defeat stung, she reflected on it and said, "Maybe I did not make the record of my career."

While she went on to create massively successful albums afterward, nothing could have prepared her for the path ahead. In 2019, Taylor shared that she would be rerecording her old albums to obtain ownership of her masters. In 2021, she went all in on the *Red (Taylor's Version)* album. She even released the fan-anticipated version of "All Too Well (10-Minute Version) (Taylor's Version)." To accompany the record, she debuted a short film that she directed, and this film went on to win a 2023 Grammy for Music Video of the Year, nine years after she lost a Grammy for the same album.

While the Tao is less interested in awards and accolades and outward success, it is about trusting and honoring the flow of the universe. Taylor's journey of *Red* was at first met with industry criticism, but it went on to become a greater success than she even anticipated and "All Too Well (10-Minute Version)" is admittedly her favorite song of her entire discography. *Red* became one of the best records of her career, but it just took its own path and its own time. The Tao reminds us that it might not make sense now, but it will, and to trust the natural balance and flow of the universe.

THIS IS ME TRYING

If something isn't what you pictured it being in the moment, is there a way that you can still be present with it and trust that it's all unfolding as it should? How can you release the friction and instead continue to trust the process ahead?

MEDITATION 3

The Loudest Person This Town Has Ever Seen

For Taylor, merely showing up to a space can cause uproar, with people thinking she is being "loud" in those spaces simply for just existing. When she started attending NFL football games to support her partner, Travis, people complained about how much they were showing her on camera. She responded in an interview with TIME *magazine for her 2023 Person of the Year feature, saying, "There's a camera, like, a half-mile away, and you don't know where it is, and you have no idea when the camera is putting you in the broadcast, so I don't know if I'm being shown seventeen times or once. I'm just there to support Travis."*

THIS IS ME TRYING

The Tao invites us, as Taylor does in her music and life, to look beyond surface judgments and hold fast to the soul of who we are. In what ways have you measured your worth by the outside and how can you instead fulfill the space within?

In her song "Anti-Hero," Taylor shares a lot of her deepest insecurities, specifically around her life being unmanageable and how it can be hard for others in her life (although she assures us not to feel bad for her!). In discussing the track on her social media, Taylor said, "You know, I struggle a lot with the idea that my life has become unmanageably sized, and that I, you know . . . not to sound too dark, but, like, I struggle with the idea of not feeling like a person."

For Taylor, trying to maintain her own sense of self can be challenging, especially given the chaos that can often follow her in life. This tension—between the outside noise and her inner world—mirrors what the Tao reminds us: True worth is not found in appearances, external measures, or fancy things, but in the spirit within. The *Tao* shares that a jar is formed from clay and a room is made of walls, but both are useless if the space is empty. In the same way, our lives may appear dazzling from the outside, but what gives them value is the fullness of the self within.

MEDITATION 4

Rid Any Bad Blood When You Can

In a 2014 Rolling Stone *interview, Taylor shared a bit behind the inspiration for her song, "Bad Blood" on the* 1989 *album. She said it was about a fellow female pop star that she thought she was her friend, but always left interactions questioning that. She then said that this person stole dancers from under her for her upcoming tour and how she realized that no, they were not in fact friends like she thought. While Taylor didn't name any names in the interview, the Internet sleuths took it by storm and eventually concluded that her comment was about Katy Perry, and the feud had begun.*

For several years, there was online drama and chatter about the two until finally, in May 2018, Katy sent Taylor a literal olive branch while she was on her Reputation Stadium Tour as a gesture that it was time to move on. Taylor took to Instagram and shared the photo that said, "Thank you Katy," with a caption that read, "So I just got to my dressing room and found this actual olive branch. This means so much to me."

Then in 2019, Taylor invited Katy to be featured in a cameo for the "You Need to Calm Down" music video. Toward the end of the video, Katy is dressed up as a burger and Taylor is dressed up as fries, and the two hug it out, signaling that they have officially squashed the beef after years of bad blood.

Holding on to grudges or having bad blood only disrupts your own flow and causes a lot of stress and anxiety. The Tao suggests that even when someone wins a legal battle, oftentimes, that bitterness still lingers. The Tao reminds us to not keep score and, instead, to forgive. The *Tao* teaches that the wise do not dwell on what others owe them or what they perceive others owe them and instead focus on their own part in restoring balance. Offering or accepting an olive branch is this very act; it is about choosing harmony for both parties rather than continuing down a destructive and bitter path.

THIS IS ME TRYING

Is there someone you need to extend an olive branch to or squash the beef with? Instead of ranting on about the same old bitter things, is there a way you can release and choose harmony for all?

MEDITATION 5

A Woman of Her Word

In a TIME *interview, Taylor discussed her preparation for The Eras Tour and said, "I know I'm not drinking on tour. I know I'm working out in between shows. I know I'm keeping my strength and stamina up. I know I'm going on that stage whether I'm sick, injured, heartbroken, uncomfortable, or stressed," she said. "That's part of my identity as a human being now. If someone buys a ticket to my show, I'm going to play it unless we have some sort of force majeure."*

Taylor has built a big reputation for her unwavering commitment to her fans, and to date, she has only ever canceled a handful of shows, all because of situations beyond her control. The first show Taylor ever canceled was in Bangkok, Thailand, during The Red Tour. The stop was canceled due to political unrest in the country. She then canceled Lover Fest in 2021 due to the COVID-19

THIS IS ME TRYING

When disruption arises causing you to cancel all your plans, reflect on how you can honor those commitments with balance and flow, returning to them when it is safe to do so. Like the calm after the storm, reflect on how you can return to that same ease.

pandemic. And, most recently, she canceled three shows in Vienna on The Eras Tour due to a terrorist plot by ISIS.

The handful of shows she needed to cancel because of an illness she immediately postponed for a later date, and she stayed true to those commitments. When given a choice, Taylor has always chosen to postpone first, ensuring she can make up the date to fans. Her commitment to her fans has made her one of the few artists with the lowest percentages of show cancellations. This dedication signaled to fans that when they buy a ticket to her concert, she and her team will do everything in their power to show up and deliver an unforgettable experience to all.

Whether it's sunny or storming, the Tao reminds us that nature is unpredictable and can cause disruption, but it also has a beautiful way of returning to peace. Storms pass, winds break, and rain turns to sunshine. The chaos and disruption are temporary. If we let go for a little while and let nature run its natural course, we can return to what we've committed to and trust that the timing is just right.

ABIGAIL BFF FIFTEEN

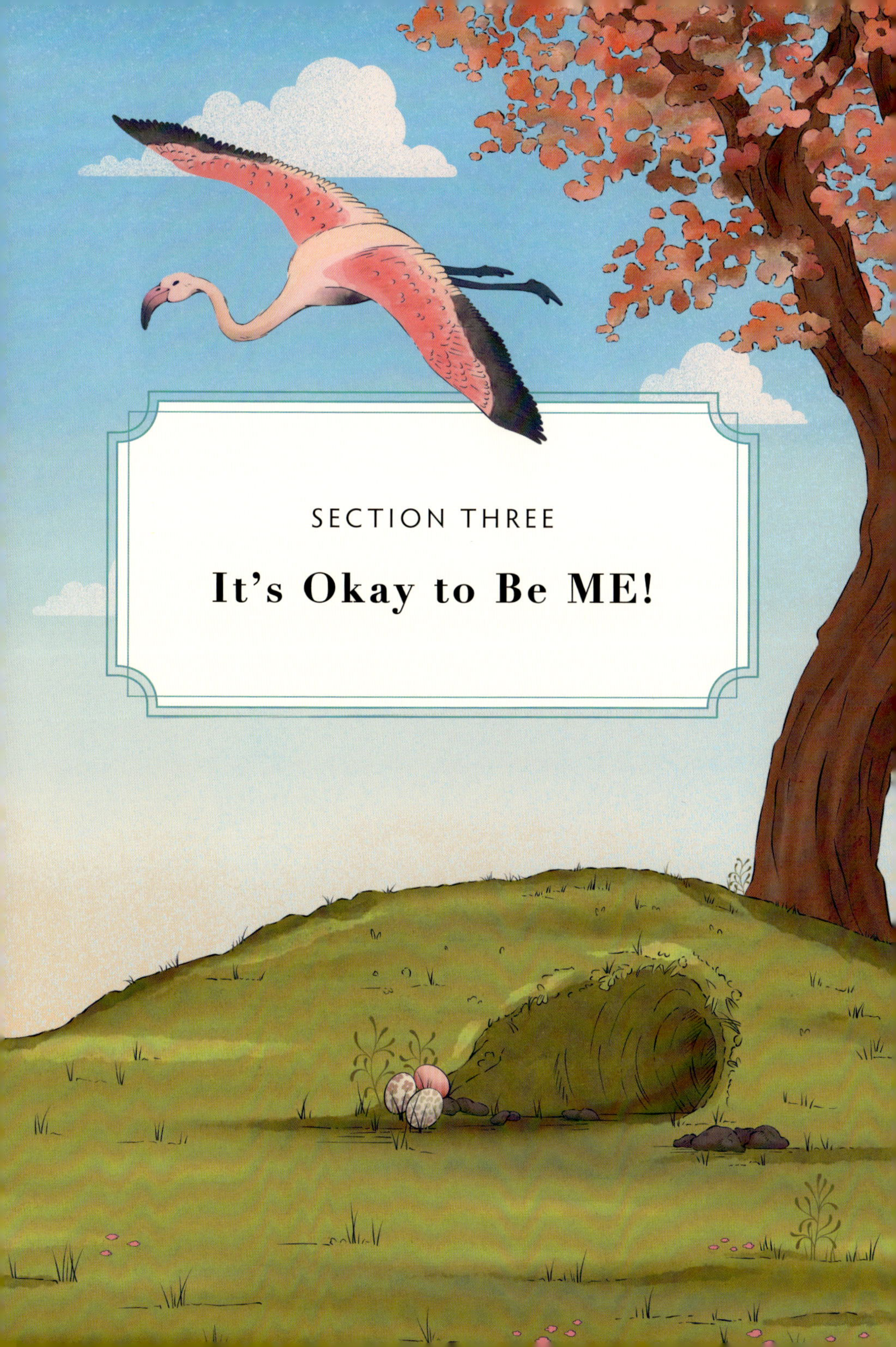

SECTION THREE

It's Okay to Be ME!

Only when there is no competition will we all live in peace.

THE *TAO*, CHAPTER 8

The worst kind of person is someone who makes someone feel bad, dumb, or stupid for . . . being excited about something. I don't think you should ever have to apologize for your excitement; just because something's cliché doesn't mean it's not something that's awesome.

TAYLOR

In the Tao, *the word* "ziran" *is the concept of being authentic and naturally yourself. When you are in this natural state, it allows effortless action to arise. The Tao serves as a reminder that it's not about forcing yourself to fit into a box of what anyone else thinks you should be, but instead it's about leaning in and flowing with what feels natural to you. And when you bring out the best in yourself, you will naturally inspire others to bring the best, fullest versions of themselves.*

We see this concept play out from the beginning of Taylor's career until present. Taylor has always been a goofy, weird, quirky person, who also happened to be a pop star. In fact, her authenticity is what made her connect and relate to so many and what helped her pop stardom rise.

In an interview with *CBS This Morning*, Taylor says, "My life doesn't gravitate toward being edgy, sexy, or cool. I just naturally am not any of those things." When asked what she is then, Taylor says, "I'm imaginative, I'm smart, and I'm hardworking. And those things are not necessarily prioritized in pop culture." She was never trying to be a "cool" girl, but rather, she was more interested in being authentic herself.

Since the beginning of her career, Taylor has always leaned in to her quirks—from sharing goofy clips of her cats or at home videos of her racing her brother (yes, both adults) to see who can find the most Easter eggs on Easter. Her mom even leaked her infamous "Lasik eye" video to *The Tonight Show with Jimmy Fallon*. The video shows a loopy Taylor, with goggle-like glasses tapped to her eyes, crying over a banana. It then pans to a shot of her trying to eat the banana in her bed. Her mom warns her to sit up and be careful that she doesn't fall asleep and she responds, "I'm not asleep, my mind is alive."

Whether it's her quirky captions, her stage banter, her ability to laugh at herself, or her cat-lady persona, Taylor Swift embodies the concept or "*ziran*." And in a world of comparison and labels, both Taylor and Taoism remind you that you already belong, exactly as you are, weirdness, quirks, and all. The longevity in her career and the connection to her fans is a testament that if you continue to be yourself, people will see the real you. In fact, her weirdness is what truly makes her . . . her! And that's what makes you . . . you! The fun of all of us is that we have quirks and qualities that make us uniquely us. That is the beauty of the Tao.

MEDITATION 1

Be a Chewbacca

During the Red era, Taylor was interviewed on The View, *and she shared that for Halloween one year in high school, she and her best friend, Abigail, noticed that a lot of the students at her school were going as a "sexy" version of something like a teacher or a police officer. Instead of doing what everyone else was doing, the pair decided to "go full-on Chewbacca," hairy face masks and all.*

In fact, Taylor has rocked some interesting Halloween costumes over the years. In 2015, she posted a throwback photo of a young Taylor dressed as the yellow Teletubby, Laa-Laa, with the caption, "When you dress as the yellow Teletubby for Halloween, but it's before Teletubbies got huge so all the kids at school ask you why you're dressed as a yellow pregnant alien."

THIS IS ME TRYING

Have you ever tried to shape yourself into something you're not? What would it look like, instead, to flow with the things that make you . . . you! Find the quirks and traits that belong to you and embrace them. In fact, how can you bring more of yourself and who you are to your life? Are there areas that you held back on for fear of looking silly? Don't be afraid to go full-on Chewbacca in your own life.

On her *1989* tour, Taylor performed on Halloween and dressed up as Olaf from *Frozen* during her song "Style." She has been a bear, a squirrel, Spider-Man, and Ariel from *The Little Mermaid*. In all her costumes, Taylor leans in to her quirk and doesn't take herself too seriously. From the Teletubby to Chewbacca to a squirrel, Taylor embraces her weirdness and in turn gives others permission to do the same.

While Taylor's career has evolved, she never let go of her playful and quirky side. Playfulness and spontaneous acts like dressing for Halloween and not taking yourself too seriously are part of the Tao's essence of embracing natural authenticity. The *Tao* reminds us that nature does not play favorites based on merit or "coolness"—after all, a carnation isn't less sacred than a rose. Both belong and it's a reminder that our quirks make us who we are and part of the larger connected world.

MEDITATION 2

You Can Be Multi-Passionate

When looking to create the music video for "The Man," Taylor reached out to female directors, but everyone she reached out to was booked, so she decided that maybe she could direct the video herself. Not only was this the first video that she directed, but she also wrote the script, wrote the song, and starred in it (yes, as THE man).

In an interview on *Variety*'s Directors on Directors series, Taylor was asked if directing had ever been one of her career goals. She said, "No," and explained, "I have always written stories, poetry, songs. And I think this just grew out of that storytelling. And the more I did it, the more I loved it."

Try to put her in a box all you want, but Taylor has proved time and time again that you can contain multitudes and be multi-passionate. She's a singer, songwriter, businesswoman, boss, ghostwriter, director, screenwriter, and an actor, just to name a few of her roles. However, that doesn't stop her from trying new things she is excited about. She continues to go where the flow of her career leads her.

Naturally, we are all multifaceted creators. We like different things. We might even have conflicting views. We change our minds. We switch careers. All of this is because we contain multitudes and dualities. Within us are what might seem like opposing forces, but the *Tao* reminds us that they blend together seamlessly and are a natural part of the world and who we are.

THIS IS ME TRYING

If you feel boxed in by the labels people put on you and your career or talents, this is a reminder that it is okay to be multi-passionate and try new things. You don't have to stick to one thing. It doesn't make you flighty or flaky just because you want to do something new. What are some ways you can find that inner trust as you take the next step of your journey?

MEDITATION 3

Go Down the Rabbit Hole

Easter eggs have become part of the Swiftie lexicon. From secret messages in her album liner notes to online countdowns and numerology to the details in her outfits and even her nail polish, Taylor keeps things fun for fans by creating an interactive experience with her art.

Discussing the use of Easter eggs, Taylor said it started as a way to incentivize her fans to read her lyrics, which she is the proudest of. She then said it got a bit out of control once she realized how much fun her fans were having with it, too, and she couldn't stop. Sharing about Easter eggs on *The Tonight Show Starring Jimmy Fallon*, Taylor said, "I think that it is

THIS IS ME TRYING

If you are used to doing things the same way, how can you instead practice a bit of spontaneity to keep things interesting? Go on a spontaneous date night by giving your partner scavenger clues as to what's next. If you are creating a new product, see if there is a way you can infuse something super interesting and unique into it. If you always take the same route every single day, maybe try a new route and notice the new things that you see.

personally reasonable for people to be normal music fans and to have a normal relationship with music. But if you wanna go down the rabbit hole with us, come along. The water's great. Jump in."

Spontaneity and playfulness are part of the Tao. It's about actions that feel fluid and not forced. It's about being open to the journey and where it leads rather than fixating on the outcome of it. Although Taylor started the Easter eggs as a way to get people to really read the lyrics, they quickly took on a life of their own, and the outcome led somewhere completely different. And much like the Tao, the water is great if you just let it keep flowing naturally.

MEDITATION 4

Embrace Your Cat-Lady Persona

In a 2014 interview on Live with Kelly & Michael, *Taylor talked about her cats, Meredith Grey and Olivia Benson, and said, "Before I got the second cat, I was kind of canvassing everyone I knew, saying, 'Is* cats, cat lady?*' Two cats is* cats, *and there's more than one. And they're like, 'No, three cats is a cat lady, two cats is a party.'"*

Then, in 2019, Taylor officially cemented her status as an official "cat lady" when she adopted her third cat, Benjamin Button, when she met him on the set of her music video, "ME!" A few years later, during photo shoots for 2023 *TIME* Person of the Year magazine covers, Taylor famously wore Benjamin around her neck like a scarf, taking her cat-lady persona to the next level.

Her cats can be seen traveling with her and on Instagram videos, and she mentions them in everything from songs and music videos to interviews and commercials. She even went to cat school to learn how to transform into a cat on the big screen for her role in the movie *Cats*! And as she has lovingly reminded us, "You can't spell *cats* without TS."

If you love something, embrace it. Taylor has taken on the persona of being a "cat lady" and embraced it. While society has often used the phrase "cat lady" as a limiting or mocking label targeted at older, unmarried women who have a lot of cats, Taylor is showing that loving cats is not a bad thing and it's part of what makes her . . . her. The *Tao* reminds us that everyone has their own likes and dislikes that are true to us. And when we release the need for others to act according to our own likes, desires, or expectations, we can be more authentic to ourselves and more respectful of others.

THIS IS ME TRYING

Embrace your inner "cat lady"—whether you have a cat, love cats, or just want to live more authentically: find the thing that you care about and embrace it. Lean in to the things you enjoy and care about with intention and joy.

MEDITATION 5

Lean In to Your Weirdness

Taylor's playful goofy weirdness has captivated her fan base and created a playful relationship over the years. In an interview talking about her fans, she said, "I really care about their opinions and their theories and their teasing and their mocking and their joking. It's all from a very loving place."

Her weirdness shines through her interviews, her music videos, her online profiles and captions, and even moments caught on camera that she didn't see coming. Like when she chest-bumped a friend at an NFL football game or when she was singing "I Believe in a Thing Called Life" in the stands at a US Open match.

THIS IS ME TRYING

It's okay to be a little bit weird! Think about some of your weird quirks—how can you lean in to them more? Or, in what areas of your life can you lighten up and find some levity?

She is weird in other subtle ways, too. Like her "Kitty Corner" segments on *The Ellen DeGeneres Show*, her infamous *SNL* monologue song, and when she performed on "Ew" with Jimmy Fallon. She also holds a pen oddly. She draws stars in really weird shapes. (And when a fan asked her what they were she responded, "stars do u like dem").

While the *Tao* doesn't explicitly say, "Embrace your weirdness!" or "Be goofy," it does, however, say, "A living being is tender and flexible; a corpse is hard and stiff. It is the same with everything—leaves and grass are tender and delicate, but when they die they become rigid and dry." In other words, lighten up because if you don't, you're dead. Don't take things too seriously. Levity and lightness help make flowing through life easier and more enjoyable.

A Lot Going On at the Moment

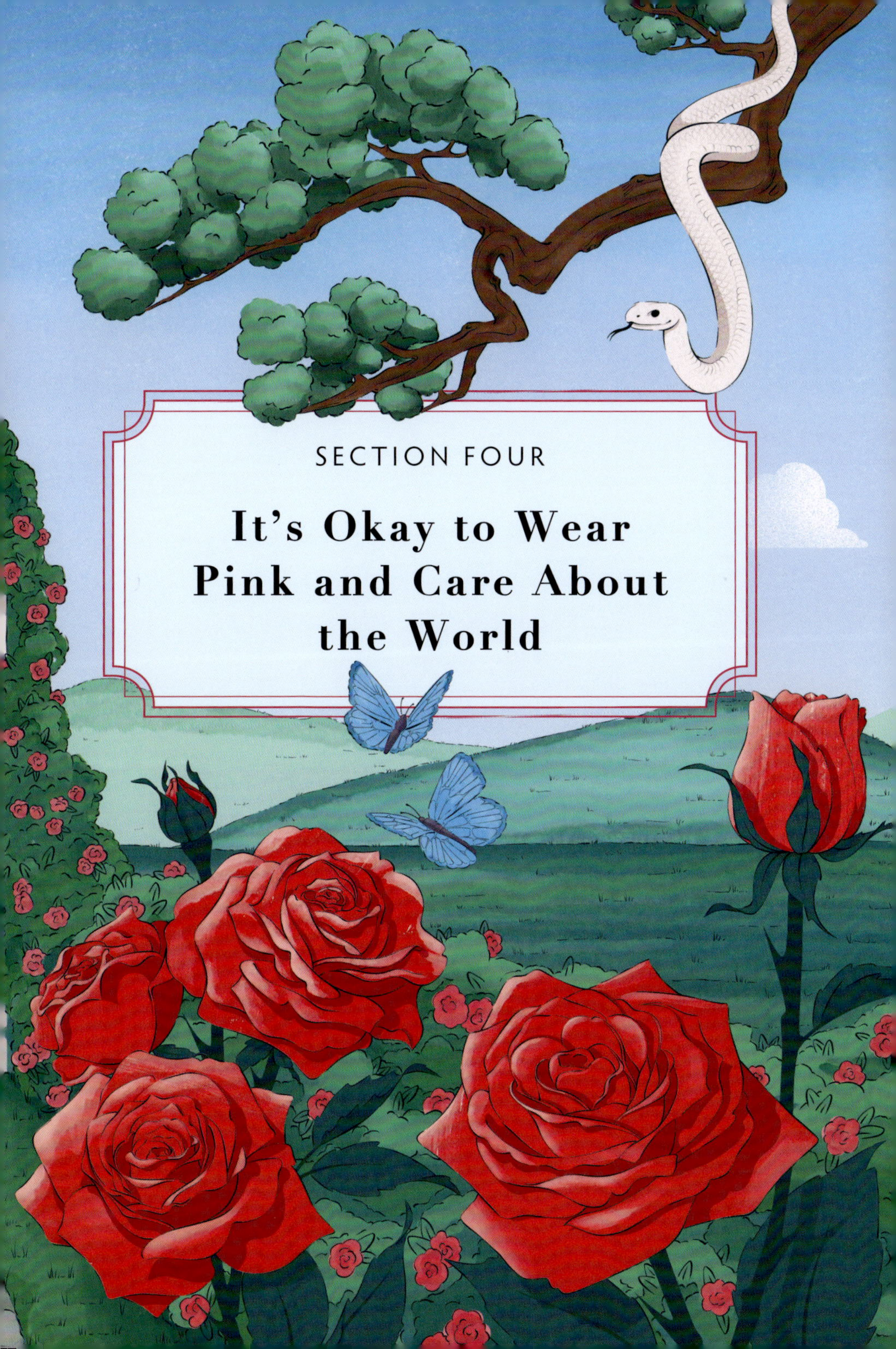

SECTION FOUR

It's Okay to Wear Pink and Care About the World

All things carry Yin yet embrace Yang. They blend their life breaths in order to produce harmony.

THE TAO, CHAPTER 42

I wanna love glitter and also stand up for the double standards that exist in our society. I wanna wear pink and tell you how I feel about politics. I don't think those things have to cancel each other out.

TAYLOR

Was it accidental or am I a mastermind? Is this a fairytale or isn't it? Taylor is also no stranger to the duality that exists in her world, from her personal life to her lyrics. She both wants to be in the spotlight for her career while also having the privacy of her personal life. Her albums go from country to pop to folk. She has songs that get you dancing around your room when the night ends to songs that have you down bad crying at the gym. Those are just a few examples, but who's counting? (One, two, three . . .)

In Taoism, these dualities are known as yin and yang. Yin is passive and reflective while yang is active and expressive, but both contain tiny dots of each other, often expressed through the popular black and white yin and yang symbol that you likely had as a keychain or necklace growing up. These two seemingly opposite forces actually transform into one another—winter becomes summer, days turn into nights, and rest transforms into action.

Just like the Tao, we too contain multitudes. We can go in and out of those dueling energies—happy, free, confused, lonely, miserable, and magical. We see this in nature as well. A rose bush is absolutely beautiful but contains thorns that can pierce the skin. The thorns, however, are what protect the plant from predators to allow for the beautiful flowers to bloom. The thorns give meaning to the bloom. These opposite energies can help us find balance in our own lives or give us hindsight perspective. We are reminded that a rose garden full of thorns is still beautiful. Recognizing the yin and yang helps you see that even difficult moments, tragedies, and love lost are just temporary ripples in a larger flow of your life.

MEDITATION 1

The Archer and the Prey

Throughout Taylor's career she's been seen as the archer and she's been seen as the prey. She's been labeled "America's Sweetheart" and a villainous snake. She's been called "a single cat lady" and "a serial boy-crazy dater."

In her discography, Taylor has also leaned in to these opposite portrayals. One of the best examples of this is during her *Reputation* era. After being labeled as a "snake" on the Internet, Taylor went silent, and when she finally reemerged, she traded in the happy pop vibes of her previous *1989* album and instead leaned in to the dark, black and white imagery of her *Reputation* era, reclaiming and embracing the snake as her symbol. We see this once again when she stepped out of the *Reputation* era and glided right into the *Lover* era, where the dark snake imagery transformed once again into a colorful pastel display of butterflies.

THIS IS ME TRYING

Think of two qualities in your own life that seem to be in opposition to one another. Maybe there are times in your life when you felt resilient and others when you felt vulnerable. Maybe you were ambitious in your career and later felt the need to rest. When have you had a tight grip on something but chose to let go? Reflect on how these dualities flow through one another. Rather than thinking of them as "good" or "bad," can you see how both worked together for greater harmony?

In the *Tao-te Ching*, we learn that these opposites only exist in relation to each other and each defines and gives the other meaning. When someone labels something as "good" or "bad," these are based on human constructs. However, if we let go of these rigid judgments of self and others, we can see how there can be harmony through the opposites. These dualities are not oppositions to be solved, but they are instead a natural part of the harmony of the world.

MEDITATION 2

Happiness

What does it mean to be happy? This is a big question to answer. However, the Tao *answers it simply. Happiness is an internal state of being, embracing the present, and aligning with the rhythms of the world. Happiness doesn't mean that nothing "bad" will ever happen. It just means that both "good" and "bad" are parts of the whole, and only by allowing the flow of both can you find true happiness.*

THIS IS ME TRYING

Reflect on a relationship or situation that was part of your path to lead to where you are now. Can you find happiness in both what it was and what it is now? Can you sit with the duality of happiness?

One of my favorite examples of this is in Taylor's song "happiness" from the *evermore* album. The song reflects the opposing forces in a relationship through the lens of happiness. When you have an aerial view on a situation, like a relationship, you can start to see it for what it is and continue to move through life with gentleness and ease because you have a better perspective. However, when that weight, grief, or struggle is right beside you and you are in it, it is hard to have perspective and it's easy to resist the flow.

In the song, Taylor reflects on a relationship and how there is both happiness because of the person and the relationship and there will be happiness once again, even if the current state is filled with heartache because of the ending. The *Tao* reminds us that happiness is not something that is pursued, but rather it is something that arises as we live with the natural flow of our life, understanding that endings are, too, a part of our internal happiness.

MEDITATION 3

It's Okay to Love Glitter and Care About the World

When deciding to finally share her stance on politics, Taylor was met with resistance from people closest to her, but she had a deep desire to let people know where she stands, even if it impacts who likes her or buys her music. For years, she had said that no one wanted to hear about politics from her, they just wanted to hear her music. Plus, she grew up in a time where country artists, like The Chicks, were canceled for sharing their political beliefs. However, as the tides changed in politics, Taylor started to find her own voice and realized that she can both be a singer and care about issues she believes in.

The Tao teaches us that duality exists. You are not simply one or the other, but instead, a beautiful combination of both. You don't need to choose one identity or expression at the expense of the other. In Taoism this represents balance. It's where you can find softness and strength, joy and seriousness, and sequins and politics. They all coexist together as part of the whole.

Since sharing her political views, Taylor has continued to be an advocate for gender equality, racial equality, and LGBTQ+ rights. She's used her platform to create change, including the influx of voter registrations that were a direct result from her social media efforts. She has even put activism in her art—showing that these two things are not mutually exclusive, but instead they can actually enrich one another.

THIS IS ME TRYING

Approaching these dualities as "both/and" rather than "either/or" is the essence of the Tao. What ways do you practice "both/and" in your life, embracing life's nuance and duality? How do you balance your own version of loving glitter and caring about the world?

MEDITATION 4

Keep Making Art

Taylor's autobiographical lyrics often showcase how she turns some of her most painful moments into songs that connect deeply with her fans. ("All Too Well," or "loml," anyone?) She also turns some of her happiest and most joyful moments into songs as well. (Like "Welcome to New York" and "Long Live.") But no matter what emotion is thrown her way in her personal or professional life, Taylor does one thing: she keeps making art.

THIS IS ME TRYING

This is a reminder to keep making your art. Turn your pain, heartbreak, lessons, and discoveries into creating art, even if it is ultimately for yourself. It can be healing for you and maybe even someone else, too. What can you remind yourself when you feel like giving up on your art, passions, or interests?

In her 2023 *TIME* Person of the Year Interview, Taylor reflected on this and said, "My response to anything that happens, good or bad, is to keep making things."

During an interview with Zane Lowe, she took this reflection a bit further. She discusses advice she gives to new or younger artists who get their first bad wave of press. Her advice? "Do not let anything stop you from making art. Just make things. Do not get so caught up in this that it stops you from making art. Or if you need to, make art about this. But never stop making things."

Both good and bad experiences can fuel creation. These yin and yang opposites are not meant to stop you from creating, but rather their duality is where the source of inspiration stems. Plus, creating art and making things itself can help you tap back into the natural flow of life, continuing to transform both those dualities into artistic expression.

MEDITATION 5

Def Leppard and Taylor Swift?

In 2008, CMT hosted a show called Crossroads *in which they paired a country star with artists of other genres, hosted a musical mash-up, and aired it on TV. A young Taylor, who just launched her debut album, was paired with Def Leppard. A classic rock band from the 80s and a teen country music star—what could they possibly have in common?*

Joe Elliot, lead singer and founder of Def Leppard said, "People were looking at us like we had three heads when we announced we were going to do this TV show with Taylor Swift. The point is to get two extremely opposite artists performing on it . . . we just saw it as an opportunity to do something different. And it was phenomenal fun."

This isn't the only one of her collaborations that might seem a little opposite. Taylor also performed a parody of her song "Love Story" with T-Pain, called "Thug Story," at the 2009 CMT Music Awards. She has collaborated with artists from country, pop, indie, classic rock, emo, rap, and more.

Oftentimes, we are quick to judge opposing forces, thinking that in no way could the two fit so seamlessly together. I'm sure that has been said about peanut butter and jelly, chocolate and pistachio, or chicken tenders and seemingly ranch. However, the Tao is a constant reminder that though they might seem opposite in nature, they are not experienced as opposites.

In the case of Def Leppard and Taylor? We see the classic rockers bringing the yang energy, intense and edgy. And we see Taylor as the yin force, soft and resonant. Together, they create an unexpected balance and harmony—not to mention a great show that both fanbases could enjoy.

THIS IS ME TRYING

The Tao reminds us that opposites are not enemies but complements, each giving meaning to the other. Where in your own life can you welcome both sides of an apparent contradiction or weird pairing, and instead, allow their balance to create something magical?

BEST DAY

SECTION FIVE

The Little Things Are the Big Things

Love the whole world
as if it were your self;
then you will truly care
for all things.

THE TAO, CHAPTER 13

I think it's important to be self-aware about what people are saying about you, but even more so, be very aware of who you actually are, and to have that be the main priority.

TAYLOR

The word “pu” *means an “uncarved block of wood,” and it is often used as a metaphor in Taoism. An uncarved block of wood showcases both simplicity and potential. The uncarved wood is simple and beautiful on its own and it can also be transformed into other items like floors, benches, tables, and more. Neither is good or bad or better than the other as they all started from the same uncarved wood. Simplicity is not emptiness, rather it is the richness of appreciating what already is and who you are, like both Taylor and the Tao remind us.*

While Taylor's life is surrounded by paparazzi and can often be seen through the glitz and glam of award shows, photoshoots, and sequined outfits, Taylor reminds us that while people will try to shape us through expectations, labels, and critiques about who we are, ultimately, what matters most is the wholeness that we all already have before being shaped by the people and world around us.

To connect and stay grounded in who you are, the Tao celebrates the simplicity, stillness, and peace that comes from the quieter moments in life. The "best days" are often a patchwork quilt of unassuming moments like antique shopping with your family or sharing quiet times at home.

While Taylor might be on a world stage, she's still a girl from rural Pennsylvania excited to bake a loaf of sourdough and play Scrabble with her friends and family. These small moments provide us with space and stillness to connect with ourselves and recognize who we truly are. While the uncarved block of wood can be shaped into something, there is the constant reminder of the beauty of what it has been all along.

MEDITATION 1

Holy Ground(ed)

For a pop superstar like Taylor Swift, who has been in the spotlight since she was a teen and lived the life of a showgirl—lights, cameras, adoring fans, and even media frenzies—it seems like staying grounded would be a difficult task. However, in interviews with friends of the pop star, most are quick to comment on how seemingly normal and down-to-earth Taylor is.

Her friend Zoë Kravitz commented about Taylor on *The Tonight Show Starring Jimmy Fallon*, saying, "What is weirder to me, actually, is that after she performs for however many thousands of people, she just comes over after and we, like, drink some wine, eat a burger, and hang out. You would just never know that she'd just performed at Wembley. There are

THIS IS ME TRYING

What are subtle ways you might be trying to stand taller around others? How, instead, could you ground yourself and learn to walk alongside others to find more balance and peace?

a lot of famous people who don't let you forget that they're famous. They bring Wembley home with them; she really just turns into a normal person. It's pretty crazy."

In an *ExtraTV* interview, Taylor was asked what helps her stay grounded. She said, "I watch other people and their storylines and their life and how you know I would watch *Behind the Music* growing up and I would really notice the first thing, the first step of someone's decline in life and in their career was when they lost perspective and they started seeing themself as being smarter than everyone else, or cooler than everyone else, or bigger or better. And I always saw that as being the greatest misstep someone can have in their career, so I just focus really hard on just constantly reminding myself of what is important."

The *Tao* reminds us that appearing "above others," like self-display, self-inflation, and self-assertion, is unhealthy and creates an imbalance. True grounding comes from humility, from walking gently and steadily with others. And like Taylor reflects, it's about reminding ourselves what is truly important and keeping sight of that.

MEDITATION 2

Return to the Root

In an interview with NME *magazine, Taylor said, "I'm in the news every single day for multiple different reasons, and it can feel, at times, if you let your anxiety get the better of you, like everybody's waiting for you to really mess up and then you'll be done. A lot of the time I need to call my mom and talk for a really long time, just to remind myself of all the things that are great and all the things that matter."*

Her song "The Best Day" was written for her mom and reflects on how her mom has always been a grounding presence, from childhood to touring as a teenager to dealing with bullies at school and all the moments in between. On a special Mother's Day post on social media, Taylor said, "My conversations with my mom have always been and will always be some of my favorite memories—from when I was ten months old in this video from October 1990 to now talking every day on the phone. Our talks are everything to me."

During times of anxiety, the Tao teaches us to return to the nurturing root source, that stillness of life. For Taylor, calling her mom and talking is one of the ways that she does this. We see the importance of this throughout her career, as her family, especially her mom, are a big source of grounding stillness for her.

THIS IS ME TRYING

Just like a Christmas tree or a willow tree, when grounded and rooted with the people who matter most, it can help you to bend without breaking, change without losing, and grow with grace and care. Being rooted is not rigid, but rather it keeps us connected to what matters most. Who can you call or lean on when you need to feel rooted?

MEDITATION 3

It's Nice to Have a Friend

Taylor often discusses how she didn't have many friends as a little kid. In fact, she was often seen as an outsider and had trouble fitting in. As a teen, she met a redhead named Abigail in her freshman English class and, before you know it, the two of them were best friends, and they remain best friends to this day. Abigail was even the inspiration for the song "Fifteen."

However, as Taylor grew in the spotlight, so did her friend circle. She started being seen with actresses, models, and other famous folks, who became known as the infamous "squad." However, Taylor later admits that this "squad" was definitely a reaction to her childhood wounds of not having friends. She reflects on this in a 2019 *Elle* magazine essay and says, "In my twenties I found myself surrounded by girls who wanted to be my friend. So I shouted it from the rooftops, posted pictures, and celebrated my

THIS IS ME TRYING

How can you honor the friendships that have come and the ones that have gone, knowing that they were all part of your ever-flowing path?

newfound acceptance into a sisterhood, without realizing that other people might still feel the way I did when I felt so alone. It's important to address our long-standing issues before we turn into the living embodiment of them."

Friendships in the Tao are kind of like two rivers meeting—they meet (often because of other friends or mutual interests or pure chance) and then flow together through life. The best friendships aren't forced, but continue to flow with natural ease. Others might flow and lose each other, but find their way back with little effort. And others might part ways for good. However, each friendship makes up the greater flow of the river all together and their ripples are still a part of us.

Taylor shares this Taoist sentiment in that same essay, where she said, "Something about 'we're in our young twenties!' hurls people together into groups that can feel like your chosen family. And maybe they will be for the rest of your life. Or maybe they'll just be your comrades for an important phase, but not forever. It's sad but sometimes when you grow, you outgrow relationships. You may leave behind friendships along the way, but you'll always keep the memories."

Friendships, like the Tao, move. Some are here for a season and others are rooted deeply. We have seen this movement in Taylor's friendships that have come into her life in different eras. While some friendships fade and some remain, all leave an imprint on our story.

MEDITATION 4

It's a Loaf Story

Not only is Taylor a decorated artist, but she is also a talented cook. Her friends have always raved about her meals and how she loves cooking when she has them over. She's baked cookies for fans during her Secret Sessions. She's brought homemade pastries to NFL games for the football players and gifted her infamous sourdough to friends and family. And one of her favorite go-to dishes when friends come over? Ina Garten's Real Meatballs and Spaghetti (Taylor just uses packaged breadcrumbs and only ground beef for the meat). She even graced the Internet with her famous Chai Sugar Cookies recipe so all could enjoy it at home.

Taylor shared how her love of cooking changed and how it became an act of self-care. She said, "I was in my teens, and my life revolved around touring. On my rare days off at home, I barely ever cooked because it had always felt like a chore. Watching Ina prepare a meal changed my perspective on cooking and reframed it as something relaxing. She made cooking feel like self-care. Ever since, cooking has been my escape from stress and one of the only ways I can truly calm myself on a rough day. I'll always be grateful to her for giving me that."

Cooking is a wonderful metaphor for the Tao. It often starts with simple ingredients. Take bread for example; with just simple ingredients such as flour, water, salt, yeast, and sugar, it can transform into a crusty, wonderful loaf of nourishing bread. And dough rising? It's usually on its own timing, much like the Tao. Plus, cooking can transform us. By kneading dough, simmering sauces, and experimenting with flavors, we can find nourishment in the act of creating.

THIS IS ME TRYING

Dust off your cookbooks and find a new recipe you can make or share with someone in your life. Let this act of care not only nourish you in the creation, but also the person (or people) you share it with.

MEDITATION 5

Remember Where You Came From

Taylor grew up in the small rural Pennsylvania town of Wyomissing, near Reading. Raised on a Christmas tree farm, Taylor's job growing up was removing the Praying Mantis from the trees to prevent them from hatching in people's homes. She gives special shoutouts to her upbringing on various song tracks, including "Seven" and "Christmas Tree Farm."

In 2011, after the success of several albums, Taylor donated six thousand books to the Reading Public Library, and the librarians were given the choice of what books to bring in. Since 2009, she has continuously visited local hospitals,

THIS IS ME TRYING

Think about where you came from. What keeps you rooted and connected to that place? What values shaped you and how can you ensure those stay planted no matter what comes your way?

singing, dancing, and creating videos with families to make their days a little brighter. And at an NFL football game, Taylor could be seen cleaning up cups and trash in the suite, attempting to leave it better than when she came.

The *Tao* reminds us that "plants blossom for a season, then return to the root." And in returning to the root, we find stillness or tranquility. While success and change are a part of the natural flow of life, the Tao reminds us to return to our roots and the stillness, to keep us connected to our inner truth.

Taylor once said, "No matter what happens in life, be good to people. Being good to people is a wonderful legacy to leave behind." We see this in the countless examples Taylor has shown us over the years—from the infamous Eras Tour staff bonuses to the kind moments shared or caught on camera, not intended for anyone else's view. She reminds us that no matter how much we evolve or what we accomplish, remembering where we came from and staying connected to our roots can keep us grounded, authentic, and in a natural flow.

SECTION SIX

Always Believe in Your Wildest Dreams

Things come her way
and she does not stop them;
things leave and she lets
them go.

She has without
possessing, and acts without
any expectations.

THE TAO, CHAPTER 2

To me, "fearless" is not the absence of fear. It's not being completely unafraid. To me, fearless is having fears. Fearless is having doubts. Lots of them. To me, fearless is living in spite of those things that scare you to death. Fearless is getting back up and fighting for what you want over and over again . . . even though every time you've tried before, you've lost. And when someone apologizes to you enough times for things they'll never stop doing, I think it's fearless to stop believing them. I think allowing yourself to cry on the bathroom floor is fearless. Letting go is fearless. No matter what love throws at you, you have to believe in it. That's why I write these songs. Because I think love is fearless.

TAYLOR

Have you ever met someone in your life and it felt like fate? The timing, circumstances, and energies all aligned, begging the question, "What if none of this was accidental?" In the Tao, nothing is accidental, but not because things are preplanned, but instead, everything unfolds exactly as it will and on its own timing. Every coincidence, every encounter, every heartbreak—they are all part of the same current. The Tao doesn't necessarily believe it was pre-destined, but more, those encounters give meaning to your life's journey and path. Even if that relationship ended or the situation changed, those encounters have meaning.

From a girl with a guitar and a dream to a woman touring sold-out stadiums across the world, it was as if all the planets and fates and stars aligned to make Taylor's wildest dreams come true. The reality was much more accidental.

We see that play out in Taylor's career, from meeting Scott Borchetta at the Bluebird Café and joining his new indie label to the eventual ending of that relationship. Or when Taylor connected with The National singer/songwriter, Aaron Dessner, during the COVID-19 lockdown and that brief text exchange transformed into a beautiful music relationship with the albums *folklore* and *evermore*. These chance accidental meetings all played a role in the bigger picture of Taylor's life.

The Tao is the real mastermind in all this, reminding us that when things aren't forced and you remain open, the universe will bring people and things together. Nothing can be forced or preconceived, but rather your wildest dreams have their own timing and our only role in the ever-changing flow of the tide is to remain fearless in our pursuits and to keep going.

MEDITATION 1

Embrace Your Power Moves

A clip surfaced of a rehearsal for an iHeartRadio performance, and Taylor can be seen on stage talking with her staff about the timing of her piano coming out. In this clip, she's asking how long the piano takes to get where it needs to be since the timing seems off. She is able to communicate directly and consult with her team, settling that the piano should come out thirty seconds earlier than it did. There was no yelling and no control, just treating everyone with respect and continuing on.

THIS IS ME TRYING

What type of leader are you or what type of leader do you aspire to be? Are you trying to control people and situations? Or are you direct and respectful? Take a step back and see if there are ways that you can assert power from within rather than by trying to control the situation.

Later, one of her staff explains that she does in fact have more time to get to where she needs and Taylor is relieved. The whole interaction shows collaboration and respect. While of course Taylor wants to put on an incredible performance and do her best, she doesn't treat people with force or control to get to the desired result. She listens, has a conversation, and moves forward.

Taylor is one of the most powerful people on the planet and a fearless leader; she doesn't need to control people or situations for that power. The Tao reflects that it's not about forcing specific standards (especially moral ones), but instead it's about living by example. When you live your life in harmony with the Tao, your behavior naturally influences those around you. This is why people who have worked for Taylor continue to sing her praises, many even saying that they, too, have learned how to lead better because of her.

MEDITATION 2

Take Things Out from the Vault

The vault tracks from Taylor's rerecorded albums have become an exciting surprise and a much-anticipated part of her rerelease drops. Her iconic "All Too Well (10-Minute Version) (Taylor's Version)" song inspired a short film that ended up claiming several awards and nominations from the American Music Awards, Grammy Awards, and MTV Video Music Awards. It went on to win MTV Video Music Awards for both Video of the Year and Best Direction, making Taylor the first person to win Best Direction for a self-directed work.

These vault tracks were the "discarded" songs for multiple reasons, including general album space and also overall flow on the final record. However, when Taylor rereleased her old albums to reclaim her masters, she included these "From the Vault" tracks in order to tell the entire story of the record and give fans the most from that album. Because of this, fans have embraced these vault tracks and in many instances, they became new instant classics and fan favorites.

The Tao reminds us that everything unfolds in its own rhythm and nothing is lost or wasted. Sometimes ideas stay dormant until the right time. Or sometimes, ideas spark when the conditions are right. The Tao reminds us that there is a season for everything and these ideas will bloom exactly when they are meant to. Even setbacks are part of the natural flow. Just because something didn't work right now, doesn't negate the value or potential in the future.

Just because you didn't get to use an idea right away, doesn't mean it's not good or that it's too late. You can absolutely pick up a project from years ago and breathe new life into it. On the flip side, just because something didn't succeed in the way you envisioned at first, doesn't mean it never will.

THIS IS ME TRYING

How can you continue to cultivate trust on the timing of your ideas and projects, allowing them to return or evolve without force or judgment?

MEDITATION 3

Bet on Yourself

When Taylor Swift went from country to pop in her album 1989, it came with pushback from her team. She told Billboard *magazine that one of her biggest challenges was to convince her team that switching to pop was the best move. "[My] team said, 'Are you really sure you want to do this? . . . Are you positive that you want to take a genre that you cemented yourself in, and switch to one that you are a newcomer to?' And answering all of those questions with 'Yes, I'm sure' really frustrated me at the time—like, 'Guys, don't you understand, this is what I'm dying to do?'"*

THIS IS ME TRYING

Check in on your own life and reflect on when you made bets on your gut and intuition versus when you listened to the outside voices and noises of others. Where in your life have you hesitated or stopped your flow because of others' doubt of something? How can you instead follow your own instincts and cultivate a deep trust within yourself?

Even people on her own team resisted Taylor's instincts, but instead of second guessing herself or resisting with them, she continued. She was betting on herself authentically when everyone else was resisting because of ego. While family, friends, or your team might try to impose their own expectations, the Tao is a reminder that if you act with authenticity and not ego, things will unfold naturally and right where you need to be.

Taylor has continued to bet on herself and trust her instincts, lessening the outside noise so she can tap into her internal truth and direction of her path. We see this in the documentary film *Miss Americana*, when she shares with her team how important it is for her to speak up about politics and issues she cares about. We also see this as she uses her voice to advocate for better royalty structures for artists and her journey to reclaim her masters. Even if it risked public criticism, Taylor ultimately listened to her gut and bet on herself and her values.

MEDITATION 4

Treat Your People Well

Coming off the massive success of The Eras Tour, it was reported that Taylor gave her entire staff bonuses (totaling $197 million) for all their hard work and sacrifices for helping make it a success. Everyone from her onstage and offstage crew received bonuses, from truck drivers, caterers, and the merch team to lighting and sound crews, choreographers, hair stylists, makeup artists, wardrobe techs, physical therapists, and more. During each stop of The Eras Tour, Taylor also donated to local food banks in each city as an act of kindness for welcoming her and her team into their city.

However, these acts of kindness are not new to Taylor, as this is who she has always been. After coming off the success of her first world tour during *Fearless*, Taylor was asked how she likes to spend her money, now that she has made a lot of it. Taylor, at just nineteen years old, said, "I try to take care of my band and my crew and just, you know, for me that's the most fun thing in the world, you know, rather than buying a Lamborghini, I just make sure like everyone feels like they're in the right place. You know, I make sure that everyone feels like they're really taken care of and paying them well, bonusing them well, and also fun things for me, I like being a good tipper at restaurants . . . and just random things that you do because you've been given a really really good lot in life and I am just really grateful so I try to just kind of help other people when I can."

The *Tao* shares, "The wise ruler treats the good with goodness; and treats the not-so-good with goodness, too—for goodness is its own reward." The Tao teaches us that true kindness has nothing to gain and no strategy to be had. It simply is because that is the reward.

Treating people with kindness and respect isn't about following rules or checking off an obligation or expecting something in return. Kindness is understanding that everyone is interconnected and deserves basic dignity and respect.

THIS IS ME TRYING

As you move through your own life, see how you can naturally cultivate acts of kindness without expecting anything in return. After all, kindness is most powerful when it flows naturally without expectation or performance.

MEDITATION 5

Have a Curious Mind

During a speech for the Billboard *Women in Music event, Taylor said, "The people who are the most successful in this world are the ones who don't stop asking questions, who don't stop being curious, and who don't stop searching for the truth."*

Having a curious mind helps you engage in the world without rigid force, control, or expectations. Instead, being curious helps you notice, explore, and learn, and most important, it helps you keep flowing through life with gentleness. We see Taylor's curious mind as she explores albums, lyrics, and art. As a writer and musician, she never stops learning her craft—often giving praise to folks like her guitarist Paul Sidoti and other musicians who inspire her to reach New Heights. Taylor shows us, through her words and actions, that she is always learning and that she will not ever "arrive" as an artist, but rather, she will always be an artist and continue to learn along the way.

THIS IS ME TRYING

If you have a question about something, try to find the answer. Immerse yourself in areas where you want to grow. Ask questions. Approach your next project with the same openness and wonder you had as a beginner and let curiosity take you somewhere new.

In her downtime, we also see her curiosity in her desire to learn everything she could about football when she started dating NFL football player Travis Kelce. Or when she got even more into baking and wanted to learn everything she could about sourdough. Or even when she became curious about how bands can write songs when they live all over the world. (And in case you didn't know, that curiosity led to the albums *folklore* and *evermore*.)

The *Tao* says, "The more knowledge you seek, the less you will understand," reminding us that wisdom (whether it be in our careers or mastering our sourdough starter) arises from observing, asking, and remaining open to where the answers to those curiosities could take us. As we wander throughout life, we often have more questions than answers, and that's a good place to be.

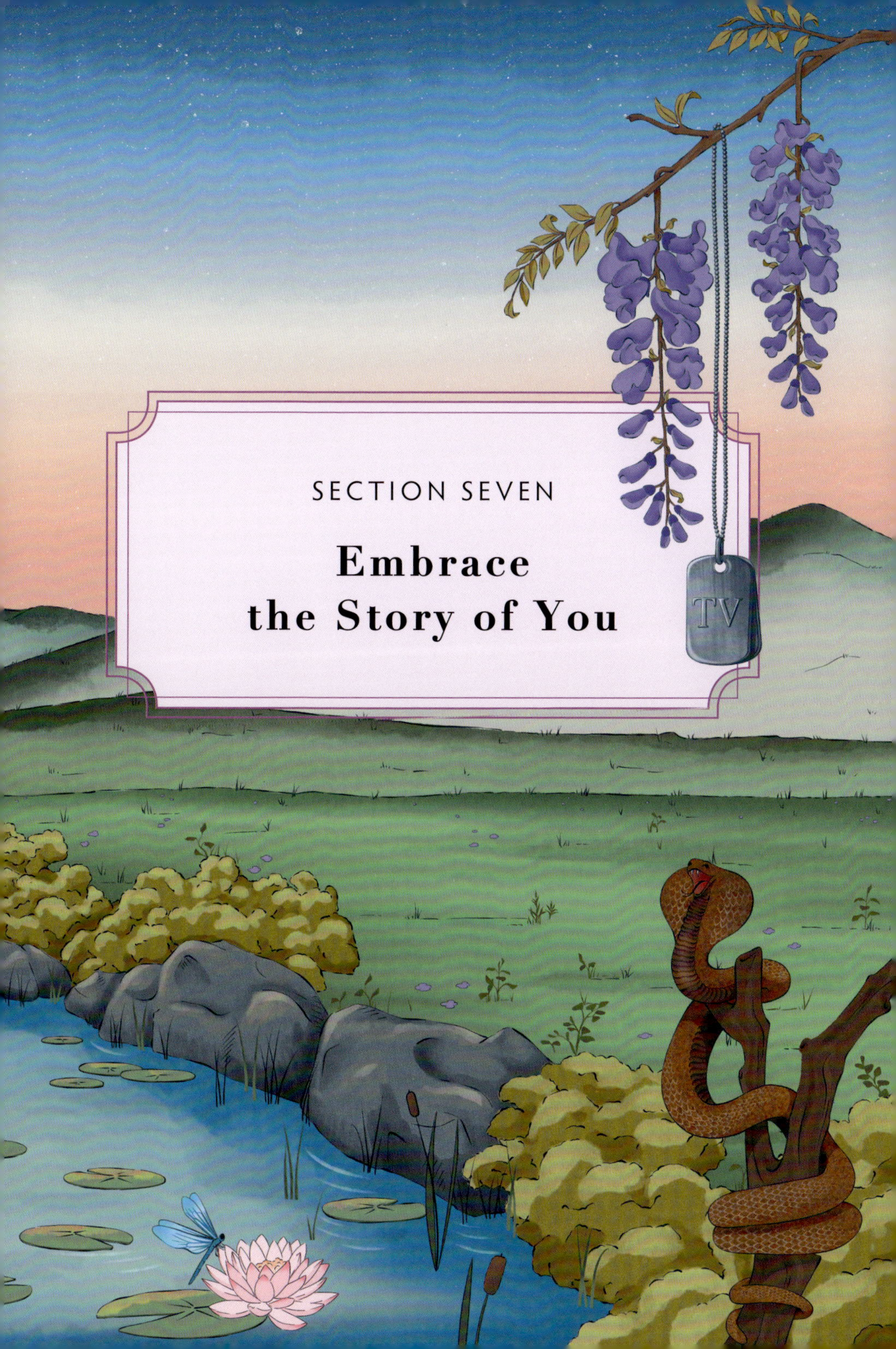

SECTION SEVEN

Embrace the Story of You

Those who know others are intelligent; those who know themselves are truly wise.

THE *TAO*, CHAPTER 33

If they don't like you for being yourself, be yourself even more.

TAYLOR

From cascading ocean blue waves to the stillness of a lake, or from open fields of lavender to crawling ivy up a stone house, nature teaches us to honor the wholeness of who we each are. After all, water can both provide waves and stillness. Flowers and plants can grow in open fields and through concrete stone. Even a crooked tree can still offer shade or provide wood for a fire. In nature, there is no competition, comparison, or judgment, each element is beautiful and purposeful on its own. Like nature, when we stop judging ourselves and others, we not only allow our most authentic self to shine through, but we in turn see that same natural goodness reflected in others' uniqueness. This is living in alignment with the Tao.

Taylor propelled into the music scene putting her authentic self out into the world. She leaned in to the things that made her unique, like her storytelling, songwriting, her love of cats, and her weird quirks. She embraced all the parts of her uniqueness. And by doing so, she inspired generations of people to do the same. Her fans saw glimpses of themself in her, and it inspired them to be more of themselves. Her concerts are safe havens where people can dress up in elaborate costumes, cry, sing, scream, and be exactly who they are without judgment.

Taylor also evolved openly and publicly, in the beginning age of social media, showing others that it's okay to change, to make mistakes, and to grow. Each era showed her evolution into where she was in life, love, and with her art. Her changes and reinventions gave others permission to change their minds, their style, their dreams, or their art, too.

Each of us has our own stories and the eras of our own life—moments of grief, joy, growth, change, love, and loss. The Tao reminds us that if we stay true to ourselves and embrace our own path, we'll find our most natural sick beat. This can't be done through forcing through the current or clinging onto things that have passed, but instead, going steady with the path, releasing what no longer serves us. Taylor reminds us of these same things through each era and each song, showing that when you stay true, the manuscript makes sense and the next chapter will, too.

MEDITATION 1

Don't Live for the Applause

Before Taylor turned thirty, she penned an essay for Elle *magazine, sharing wisdom she had learned before her noteworthy birthday. One lesson she learned was not to let outside opinions establish the value she places on her life. She said, "For too long, the projected opinions of strangers affected how I viewed my relationships. Whether it was the general Internet consensus of who would be right for me, or what they thought was "couples goals" based on a picture I posted on Instagram. That stuff isn't real. For an approval seeker like me, it was an important lesson for me to learn to have my OWN value system of what I actually want."*

THIS IS ME TRYING

Your worth is not something that is granted, it simply is. How can you learn to measure your life not by the applause from the outside, but instead, by the quiet steadiness of being true to who you are?

As someone who spent most of her life living for applause, Taylor is now reflecting on how detrimental it can be to constantly seek approval. Pleasing or approval-seeking often starts in childhood and is usually a response to criticism or bullying; it can lead to seeking approval from others so much that you become deconditioned to your own thoughts and feelings. When this happens it's easy to resist our own desires and go with what society tells us we should be or what we should be doing rather than doing what is natural to us.

The *Tao* reminds us, however, that if you continue to fill a pail after it is full, water is wasted. Or if you keep grinding an axe after it is sharp, the edge will wear away. By seeking the approval of others, no matter how hard we try, it will not yield a peaceful result. The Tao reminds us to be prudent by understanding that our values and our reputation are the things that make us . . . us. When we are rooted in our natural truth and not the made-up version we think we should be, we can move through life with flow and joy. Of course, there will be challenges, but if you are firmly planted in knowing who you are, then you can handle whatever comes your way with more ease.

MEDITATION 2

This Is Not Where the Storyline Ends

Taylor has often said that female musicians rarely have the longevity in a career that her male counterparts do and has called out these double standards through her interviews and her music.

During her album launch for *Midnights*, she was a guest on *The Tonight Show Starring Jimmy Fallon* where she laughs and says, "I'm thirty-two, so we're considered geriatric pop stars. They start trying to put us out to pasture at age twenty-five. I'm just happy to be here."

In her song "The Man," Taylor reflects on these double standards even more, pointing out everything from leadership styles to relationships to money. Going into more depth about this song in an interview with *CBS News Sunday Morning*, Taylor says, "There's a different vocabulary for men and women in the music industry, right? A man does something, it's strategic. A woman does the same thing, it's calculated. A man is allowed to react. A woman can only overreact."

The *Tao* teaches us that oppression never leads to intended results, rather it leads to more resistance. While the *Tao* doesn't address the patriarchy directly, it does teach us to release the rigid structures that can confine us because being oppressive will not work. The only reason the double standard exists is because humans impose those hierarchies. When society creates and applies these double standards, tensions naturally exist because it resists the natural flow of the universe.

THIS IS ME TRYING

We all experience these double standards at some point or another. The Tao invites us to notice these imposed hierarchies and release attachment to them. Reflect and ask yourself: Where in my own life am I enforcing or accepting double standards, and how might I return to a more balanced, natural way of being?

MEDITATION 3

Know When to Speak Now

One of the things Taylor has said time and time again, since the early beginnings of her career, is that she is a songwriter first. She has been writing her own songs since she was twelve years old. In fact, by the time she was putting her first record together, she had written more than 250 songs that she had to choose from. She has said over and over and over again that she knows she wouldn't be where she is today if she didn't write her own songs. Her writing is her deep-rooted truth and part of what keeps her going.

THIS IS ME TRYING

If you find yourself in a situation where you are rooted in your truth, but someone is trying to discredit you, can you trust that your values and actions will speak for themselves more than a loud defense could?

However, as Taylor's fame and notoriety were increasing after the success of her sophomore album, *Fearless*, so was the criticism. The media, celebs, and strangers alike started discrediting her and questioning whether someone that young wrote all those songs herself. Additionally, she had cowriters on her first two records, so people assumed that she was lying and that the cowriter likely wrote everything, with Taylor trying to take the credit for it.

While these rumors were swirling, Taylor didn't put up a fight or take things by storm publicly. Instead, Taylor took her pen and her guitar and wrote her next album, *Speak Now*, completely by herself, as the sole writer. This response was a bit of a quiet rebellion. Similarly, the *Tao* reminds us that what is rooted in the truth cannot be shaken by words (or rumors). If someone tries to discredit you, the noise will pass and what will remain is your integrity. By trusting the current of your own life and truth, eventually the false judgments and rumors will dissolve on their own. And if the noise is still there, which in Taylor's case, there is always a bit of it, knowing who you are is really all you need.

MEDITATION 4

Let Things Take on a New Life

Since Taylor's career spans over twenty years now, so many of her albums and songs have found new listeners and, in some cases, new life.

The song "Long Live" was written as a love letter to her band and crew, capturing the feeling of gratitude Taylor felt during the Fearless Tour. However, this song evolved over time and eventually became a love letter to the Swiftie fandom.

When Taylor first performed "All Too Well" live, she was battling tears because she was still full of raw emotion from the feelings that song portrayed. However, as Taylor healed and as that song became a fan favorite, she came to sing it with joy and pride.

When Taylor rerecorded *Speak Now (Taylor's Version)*, she changed a lyric in the song "Better Than Revenge" that was often seen as misogynistic, showing her growth and signaling that she was ready for this song to reflect her current values.

In all these instances, the songs took on new meanings or signified new growth in Taylor's life, and music has the power to do that. A favorite song might take on a new meaning or a lyric might hit differently depending on what season you are in.

The Tao reminds us that not everything in life is understood right away. Instead, each season unfolds in its own unique timing and lets things take on their own new life and meaning. Because when you are above the trees like a bird, you can see the situation for what it really is. However, when you are on the ground, up close to the situation, you might not be able to comprehend what it means.

THIS IS ME TRYING

Have there been moments in your life when you were looking for answers immediately, only to have them revealed to you later on? What would it look like to release the pressure to know and instead trust that perspective and clarity will come in perfect timing?

MEDITATION 5

When Life Throws You Snakes, Turn Them into Karyn

When life throws you snakes, turn them into stage art for your sold-out stadium tour. That's exactly what Taylor did after the infamous drama with a certain reality-TV star and a rapper. The duo attempted to tarnish her reputation and turn the world against her, calling her a snake on the Internet and causing a wave of people jumping on board to bully her. While Taylor retreated for about a year, when she finally returned to the spotlight, she reclaimed the snake through the imagery in her record Reputation *and even included a large blow-up display snake on the tour stage, which was lovingly named Karyn.*

THIS IS ME TRYING

When life throws you something mean someone said or did, what can you do in the moment to settle back into a sense of peace and calm? How can you continue to move forward so that it doesn't stop your own flow in life? While you might never get an apology, a letter, or even closure from that person or situation, maybe the best thing you can do is keep moving, or maybe even laugh it off.

Reflecting on this time period, Taylor said, "I learned that disarming someone's petty bullying can be as simple as learning to laugh. In my experience, I've come to see that bullies want to be feared and taken seriously." She went on to say, "It would be nice if we could get an apology from people who bully us, but maybe all I'll ever get is the satisfaction of knowing I could survive it, and thrive in spite of it."

While the *Tao* doesn't explicitly teach us how to deal with a bully, it does remind us that confronting that toxic energy with the same energy (like using fire with fire) will only feed the cycle and will ultimately stop you from reaching your own flow and peace. The way Taylor handled it? Much more in alignment with the Tao. It's about feeling the feelings while ultimately continuing to move along your own path, trusting that it will all work out.

SECTION EIGHT

Embrace the Invisible Strings

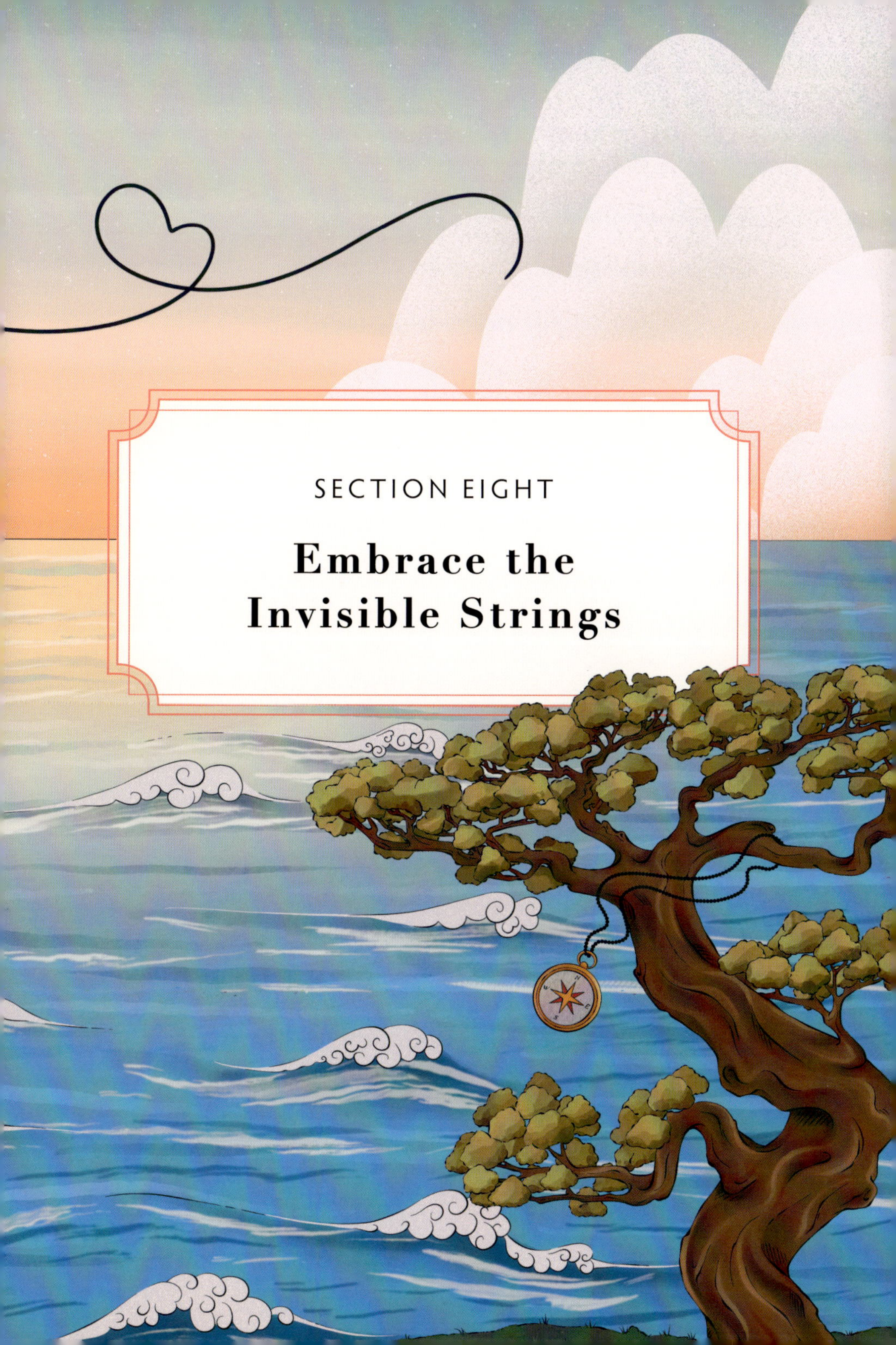

Can you remain tranquil until right action occurs by itself?

THE *TAO*, CHAPTER 15

I kind of love the romantic idea that every step you're taking, you're taking one step closer to where you're supposed to be, you know, guided by this, like, invisible string.

TAYLOR

In the Tao, there are no such things as "invisible strings" in relation to destiny pulling us toward a fixed outcome. The Tao is not a prewritten script, but instead, it is more like a river guiding our ship as long as we let go and allow ourselves to move freely with it. There is a subtle interconnected flow that unfolds when we choose to live in harmony with the current of life's flow and it's only on the reflection of our journey do we see the "invisible strings" so clearly. In Taoist terms, the invisible string isn't fate pulling you, but instead, it's the way or path expressing itself through you.

In Taylor's career, we see so many of these Taoist invisible strings that led to where she is today. What if she listened to the music executives and never released *1989* in fear of it being a flop? We wouldn't be shaking it off, that's for sure! What would have happened if she was able to buy her masters and never did her "Taylor's Version" rerecordings? We know all too well what would happen—we would have missed out on "All Too Well (10-Minute Version) (Taylor's Version)" and being able to scream along with every word while watching *The Eras Tour* (whether in person, on a grainy livestream, in theaters, or on streaming).

We also see this in her personal life. In the song, "You're on Your Own, Kid," Taylor mentions friendship bracelets in the lyrics. Creating friendship bracelets quickly hit the Swiftie fandom and trading them at The Eras Tour became a special tradition. During the stop in Kansas City, NFL Chiefs player Travis Kelce brought a friendship bracelet with his phone number on it to gift to Taylor, but he got turned away at security. He then shared the story on his podcast and the rest is history, as the two started dating shortly after and got engaged roughly two years later. However, if Taylor never wrote the song "You're on Your Own, Kid," which mentioned friendship bracelets, would that exchange have ever happened? Maybe it would or maybe it wouldn't. The Tao simply reminds us that life is naturally unfolding, and our job is to ride the vibes and the waves.

Both the Tao and Taylor's "invisible string" remind us that just like a spool of thread, if we allow it to unravel and create without force, the thread of our own story will continue to unfold and bring us right where we were meant to be.

MEDITATION 1

Permission to Fail

In 2023, Taylor won the iHeartRadio Music Innovator Award, and during her acceptance speech, she said, "But I do want to say that the thing with these exciting nights and moments and specifically this award that I'm so lucky to have gotten is that they're shining a light on the choices I made that worked out, right? The ones that turned out to be good ideas, but I really, really want everyone to know—especially young people—that the hundreds or thousands of dumb ideas that I've had are what led me to my good ideas. You have to give yourself permission to fail. I try as hard as I can not to fail because it's embarrassing, but I give myself permission to, and you should too, so go easy on yourselves and

THIS IS ME TRYING

Have you ever failed at something and then when looking back at it later, you realized that the failure led you to a future success? Maybe through a failure, you learned valuable lessons, or maybe it sparked a new idea, or maybe it encouraged you to try something different or improve your skills? Failure, like success, is neither good nor bad. Instead, they are both part of the same invisible string that leads you to right where you need to be. This is true for Taylor and it is true for you, too.

just make the right choices that feel right for you and someday someone might think you've been innovative."

The Tao doesn't see it as success versus failure. Instead, the Tao helps us see that success and failure are part of the same process and are part of one another. After all, true innovation doesn't happen because everything goes right. In fact, most innovations happen because people learned what went wrong (or what could go wrong) and used that to crack the code during the next rendition.

The Tao encourages us to lessen the grip or tension around the ideas and creations we are working on. By letting go of the fear of failure in our subconscious, our bodies and minds can relax and we can naturally flow into the next thing. Easing up can help us think better and react better, and can be the catalyst for the next great idea, transforming failures into the next creation.

MEDITATION 2

Mistakes Make You Human

In 2015, Taylor's music video for "Bad Blood" was nominated for several VMA awards. Shortly after the nominations were announced, Nicki Minaj, who was not nominated for her infamous "Anaconda" video, took to social media to comment and said, "If your video celebrates women with very slim bodies, you will be nominated for vid of the year."

Taylor, thinking this was a jab at her, responds with, "I've done nothing but love & support you. It's unlike you to pit women against each other. Maybe one of the men took your slot."

Nicki clarified that it wasn't about her and that she was missing the point. Just a few days later, Taylor publicly issued an apology to Nicki and said, "I thought I was being called out. I missed the point, I misunderstood, then misspoke. I'm sorry, Nicki."

Nicki accepted and said, "I've always loved her. Everyone makes mistakes. She gained so much more respect from me. Let's move on."

Nicki and Taylor went on to perform a mash-up of Taylor's song, "Bad Blood" and Nicki's song, "The Night Is Still Young" at the MTV Video Music Awards show, showing that there was, in fact, no more bad blood between the two.

In the Tao, mistakes are not sins or moral failures, they're a natural part of the world. The Tao doesn't punish those missteps or misunderstandings; it absorbs them, softens them, and transforms them.

Taylor shows us, through her actions, her public apology, and her willingness to admit when she's been wrong, that mistakes help us grow because they help us change for the better and change is the Tao's most constant rhythm.

THIS IS ME TRYING

The next time you make a mistake and you feel the tension in your body, stop and ask how you can soften your mistake rather than view it as a moral failure.

MEDITATION 3

thanK you

In 2019, Taylor found out that the masters of her albums were bought from underneath her, something that cut through like a knife. Instead of taking this as a defeat, Taylor decided to do something completely unconventional: She decided to rerecord all her stolen albums and rerelease them as "Taylor's Version." She originally did this for her, but it's no surprise that her fans got on board and embraced Taylor's Versions.

THIS IS ME TRYING

Fill in the blank space: If there hadn't been _____, there might not have been ____. Often, the moments that cause disruption—where we either decide to fight or decide to flow—are the ones that, looking back, we can see how they impacted us to get to where we are. For example, maybe you got rejected from your dream college or a job you really wanted. But then, it led you somewhere else altogether that feels perfect for you.

In fact, the Taylor's Version rerecordings in some instances outperformed the originals. New people were discovering her music more than ever before, and with the addition of special "From the Vault" tracks, longtime Swifties got not only new music, but also a new part of the story from records they adored.

Then, given the success of both the rerecordings and The Eras Tour, in May 2025, Taylor announced that she had officially bought back the masters to all her records. They were all now officially owned by her.

In a letter she penned about this on her website, she thanked the fans, saying, "The passionate support you showed those albums and the success story you turned The Eras Tour into is why I was able to buy back my music. I can't thank you enough for helping to reunite me with this art that I have dedicated my life to, but have never owned until now."

It's a reminder that if we lean in to what will give us peace and harmony (and we are human, so yes, some spite might also flow into that), ultimately, it carries us and leads us right to where we were meant to be.

MEDITATION 4

Loss Is Just a Step Forward

When Reputation *didn't receive a Grammy nomination and the media said the tour was going to be a "flop," Taylor responded with, "I'll just write a better record."*

Fast forward to May 2025, when Swifties were hoping for the announcement of the much anticipated release of *Reputation (Taylor's Version)* and Taylor surprised us all by announcing that she bought her masters back and officially owns all this work. In the letter she penned on her website about this, she said, "I know, I know. What about Rep TV?" alluding to the fact that fans were eagerly awaiting the rerelease and the vault tracks. In the letter, she admitted that she didn't even rerecord a quarter of it. She goes on to say, "The *Reputation* album was so specific to that time in my life, and I kept hitting a stopping point when I tried to remake it. All that defiance, that longing to be understood while feeling purposefully misunderstood, that desperate hope, that shame-born-snarl and mischief. To be perfectly honest, it's the one album in those first six that I thought couldn't be improved upon by redoing it."

Seeing this journey unfold is the perfect reminder that just because something doesn't perform up to outside standards does not mean it's not valuable. In fact, Reputation Stadium Tour was one of the best-selling tours in history and the *Reputation* album went on to be one of the most cherished albums of Taylor's discography. However, in the moment, when all you have are metrics like awards to get your feedback, it's easy to get caught up in that noise. While Taylor didn't let the story stop there, there are many people who do let those experiences make a knot in their thread, rather than continuing on and letting the thread naturally weave where it's meant.

The *Tao* asks us, Which is important or more valuable: fame or integrity, riches or good character, failure or success? The true answer is that if you are content with what you have, you will always have enough, and if you stay on your own path, you will always endure.

THIS IS ME TRYING

Rather than focusing on awards or accolades, ask yourself, "Am I proud of myself for creating this?" And if you lose something, ask yourself, "Yes, but what did I gain?"

MF

SECTION NINE

You Need to Calm Down and Breathe

The Tao never acts with force, yet there is nothing that it cannot do.

THE *TAO*, CHAPTER 37

What you spend your energy on . . . that's the day.

TAYLOR

MEDITATION 1

Sorry, I Can't Come to the Phone Right Now

In 2016, Taylor retreated from the spotlight after a public feud with Kim Kardashian and Kayne West. Reflecting on this time in her documentary, Miss Americana, *she says, "No one physically saw me for a year." Even the paparazzi weren't able to get any photographs of Taylor during that time. Then in 2017, she also went dark on social media, deleting all her old content. She unfollowed everyone on her Instagram and turned off the comments to her posts.*

THIS IS ME TRYING

Taking a break and allowing your mind to rest, whether that is a break from social media, work, or something else, can be good for your mental health, physical health, and overall creativity. Sometimes, emptying the mind and silencing the noise can help you stay present so you can come back better than you ever were before.

The Tao reminds us to take time to empty our minds and let our hearts rest, especially as we are dealing with rough currents. In Taylor's case, she did just that. She took time away from the public eye to reflect and rest.

The *Tao Te Ching* also shares, "Watch the turmoil of beings, but contemplate their return." So, while rest is important to help with your heart and mind, it's also important to take those lessons and keep going. It's about finding peace even in times of chaos and continuing on anyway. During that time, Taylor rested, but did not give up. She took her lessons and kept going, kept flowing.

She eventually resurfaced and announced her new album, *Reputation*. That restful period and contemplation ultimately helped her plan her return with more clarity . . . and a new album.

MEDITATION 2

Connect with Your Ancestors

The song "marjorie," featured on Taylor's evermore *album, pays tribute to her late grandmother, Marjorie Finlay. Marjorie was a star in her own right, a powerful opera singer known for hitting high notes and winning talent contests. She went on tour with her music and even landed a hosting gig for a variety show in Puerto Rico. In writing this song, Taylor actually found old vinyl records of her grandmother's music and featured her voice on the album, as if the two are singing together.*

In discussing adding her grandmother's vocals to the song, Taylor said, "It's moments like that on the record that just make you feel like your whole heart is in this whole thing that you're doing. It's all of you that you put into these things."

In Taosim, our ancestors are part of our path that shapes us into who we are. The Tao teaches that we are connected to everything that came before us—the Earth, the Sun, and the generations of people that have traveled and walked before us. Their lives, wisdom, and experiences—whether we met them and gleaned from them or not—flow into our own lives.

THIS IS ME TRYING

How might you be able to draw insight or guidance from those who came before you? Is there something that you feel has been preventing your own personal life flow that you need to address? Or maybe you might want to draw strength from someone down your family tree that you admire. Remember, you hold both: the things you want to carry on and the things you want to leave behind. You get to choose what's best for you.

MEDITATION 3

Breathe

Performing for three and a half hours every night during The Eras Tour is no easy feat when you are singing, dancing, and interacting with more than sixty thousand people. Taylor is a master of her craft and knows the importance of mastering her breath work. After all, Dr. Swift (yes, she got an honorary PhD from New York University in 2022) tells us to "breathe in, breathe through, breathe deep, and breathe out" in her NYU commencement speech.

While Taylor is a master at breath work, she also understands the metaphor of having space to breathe. An exhale provides

THIS IS ME TRYING

Where can you allow more breathing room in your own life? Maybe you constantly overbook yourself and could use some literal space between meetings in your calendar? Or maybe you need twenty-four hours to process a choice before you make any major decisions? Allow yourself the space you require. Give yourself a moment to breathe.

room and space in our lungs, just like having room to breathe is essential to our growth. The *Tao* reminds us that when we are confined or controlled, whether by our own internal thoughts or by external forces, we'll often resist or fight. However, when we have the extra breathing room, we have better judgment to make better decisions and grow into who we really are.

In that same speech where Taylor encouraged us to breathe, she also said, "We are led by our gut instincts, our intuition, our desires and fears, our scars and our dreams. And you will screw it up sometimes. So will I. And when I do, you will most likely read about it on the Internet. Anyway . . . hard things will happen to us. We will recover. We will learn from it. We will grow more resilient because of it."

Similarly, the *Tao* also reminds us that if we cling so hard to control or strive only to avoid failure, we will suffer instead. Yes, there will be pain, but there will also be beauty. Yes, we will screw up, but we will also recover. Just like breath work gives our bodies space, if we also give space to our mistakes, we have room to breathe and grow from them.

MEDITATION 4

Have a "Dead Day"

In discussing how she prepares for and recovers from The Eras Tour night after night, Taylor explains that she has a "dead day" in which, after the run of shows, she spends an entire day doing absolutely nothing. She said, "I do not leave my bed except to get food and take it back to my bed and eat it there."

She continues and says, "It's a dream scenario. I can barely speak because I've been singing for three shows straight. Every time I take a step my feet go *crunch, crunch, crunch* from dancing in heels. But it's the most fulfilled I've ever felt."

She rests her body before the next run of shows, but she also marvels at how fulfilled she feels even when her soles are aching. From beginning to end, Taylor put her entire being into The Eras Tour performance—her physical and mental stamina and her emotional range.

The *Tao* encourages us to be attentive at both the beginning and the end of our endeavors. At the start of something, like a project or a relationship, the energy and attention is fresh. We're usually open, curious, and focused. However, sometimes as things progress, it's easy to lose that awareness. When you hold the ending with the same reverence as the beginning, you remain in harmony with the Tao and your actions stay balanced and clear.

It's clear that Taylor was attentive to her tour not just physically—but also in the planning, care, detail, management, and execution. She accepted the fullness of The Eras Tour and was attentive from beginning to end—making it one of the most successful tours of all time.

THIS IS ME TRYING

When it comes to a goal or a project, how can you set yourself up for success, ensuring you are as attentive at the beginning as you are at the end? Maybe you need to pace yourself with rest days? Or maybe you need to be reminded of your bigger vision? Tap into those things that will support you to finish your project with the same sense of joy and attention that you started with.

MEDITATION 5

What's Next?

When a reporter asked her what she was going to do after her 1989 World Tour, Taylor responded, "I think I should take some time off. I think people might need a break from me. I'm going to . . . I don't know. Hang out with my friends. Write new music. Maybe not write new music. I don't know."

In the Tao, rest is not simply about getting good sleep and taking time off. (Although I personally recommend those things, too!) Rest is about creating stillness within and releasing the outside noises so that you can find peace and get clarity about your next steps.

THIS IS ME TRYING

The next time someone asks you "What's next?" how might you now respond in a way that honors that stillness rather than one that forces an outcome?

When Taylor launched her new album, *The Life of a Showgirl*, she was asked, "What's next?" during one of her interviews. Taylor reminded them that she just launched a new record and she was remaining present with that as her focus. In our constant hustle culture, or if we girlboss too close to the sun, resting or having downtime can make us feel guilty or not productive. However, the Tao teaches us that there is power in nonaction because that stillness allows your body and mind to tune into the world around you in a deeper way.

So often, people want to know, "What's next?" This question comes with a lot of weight to continue performing, to continue to do more, create, and be. But the Tao would likely ask the questions, "What feels true for you right now?" or "Where is your path currently leading you?" all the while knowing that it's Mr. Perfectly Fine to not know.

KM

SECTION TEN

Cultivate a Reputation of Compassion and Kindness

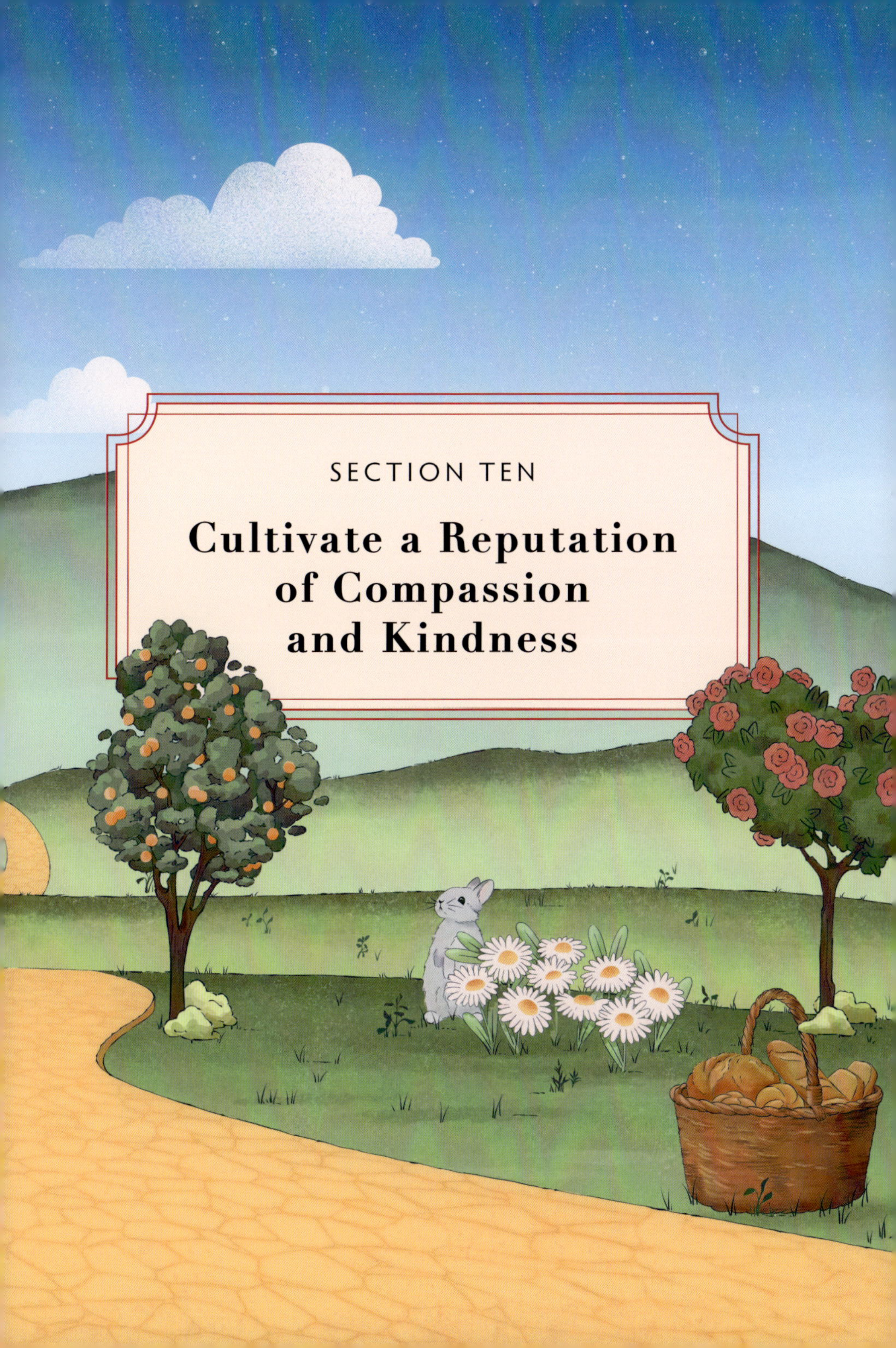

There are three jewels that I cherish: compassion, moderation, and humility. With compassion, you will be able to be brave,

With moderation, you will be able to give to others,

With humility, you will be able to become a great leader.

THE *TAO*, CHAPTER 67

I am just really grateful so I try to just kind of help other people when I can.

TAYLOR

The Tao *teaches us that compassion, kindness, and humility are courageous acts. When you are able to sit with someone in their feelings, have empathy for a situation that is outside of your own understanding, and truly feel for others, you can then find inner strength to act with courage and help others more intentionally.*

Throughout Taylor's career, we see her show up with compassion in so many different ways. In 2010, Taylor visited the Monroe Carell Jr. Children's Hospital at Vanderbilt—singing songs, signing autographs, posing for photos, and generally bringing joy to patients and families. In 2011, she turned her final dress rehearsal for the Speak Now Tour into a benefit for tornado relief, raising $750,000. In 2014, Taylor hosted "Swiftmas," in which she sent fans gifts that she hand selected based on what she knew about their interests and likes. In 2018, ahead of her Reputation Stadium Tour, she invited two thousand foster kids and their families to her final dress rehearsal, complete with a pizza party, hugs, and selfies. And a few days after ending her massively successful The Eras Tour, Taylor visited Children's Mercy hospital in Kansas City.

Donations and hospital visits aside, Taylor also shows us how compassion and kindness lead to courage. In 2014, when a young fan was being bullied online, Taylor stood up for her and sent her a heartfelt note. She sat with empathy and understanding and shared, "Every time someone picks on me, I'll think of you in the hopes that every time someone picks on you, you'll think of me . . . and how we have this thread that connects us. Let them keep living in the darkness and we'll keep walking in the sunlight. Forever on your side, Taylor."

The Taoist image of kindness is water as it flows to the lowest places, meeting and nourishing all things with compassion. Or like Taylor said, "Not to try and sound like the good witch in *The Wizard of Oz* or something, but I really do want to do good things with what I have, and that's it." When you are in alignment with the Tao, kindness naturally flows without effort and that's it.

MEDITATION 1

Ronan <3

On September 12, 2012, Taylor released a song called "Ronan" as part of a Stand Up to Cancer charity event. The song was written in honor of a boy named Ronan, who died of childhood cancer in 2011. His mother, Maya, wrote a blog journaling their story from his diagnosis to the grief of losing her son only nine months later. Taylor read the blog and became incredibly invested in their story. She used the blog as inspiration for the lyrics and the song. She not only gave Maya a writing credit on the song, but she also pledged that all the proceeds from the track would be donated to cancer charities for children.

THIS IS ME TRYING

Creating an impact is not always flashy. What are some of the quiet ways you can influence or create change? Start small with what you know.

The thing about this touching act is that Taylor did it quietly and privately. When she rerecorded *Red (Taylor's Version)*, she reached out to Maya to get her permission to include the track on this new version, cementing Ronan's story in her musical catalog forever.

The *Tao* reminds us that true strength and leadership doesn't come from force, but rather in the stillness, or quiet acts of kindness. Taylor let her compassion move through her art and did not force an agenda or an outcome. Quiet action is doing an act of kindness without ego, without pushing, and without needing to be validated for those kind actions.

MEDITATION 2

Protect the Family

Since the beginning of her career, Taylor has been a champion of small creators, artists, and businesses. She's been known to purchase handmade items on maker platforms like Etsy, she invites up-and-coming musicians to the stage, and she has hired indie artists to make custom clothing items. She even hired artist Kelsey Montague to paint a butterfly mural in Nashville as part of her release of Lover.

During the pandemic, she personally donated to her favorite Nashville record store, Grimey's New & Preloved Music, providing them with enough money to cover staff paychecks and health care for three months. Co-owner Doyle Davis said, "All my full-timers got a check, including me and my business partner—the owners—and three months of those health care costs being paid, so I know our insurance is safe. It's just huge. That gives me the peace of mind to know my people are taken care of—now I can focus on the business."

The *Tao* encourages us to see others as ourselves. To see other people, families, towns, and countries as our own. It's a reminder to see the humanity in others and to not forget where you came from. Taylor shows through her actions that she sees others as herself and is always the first to help protect the family when she can.

Seeing others as yourself can mean many different things. It can mean supporting local, independent businesses because you can understand their desire to provide for their community and family. It can mean taking time to listen to someone who thinks differently than you do. Or, it could mean leaving a place you are visiting in better condition than you found it. When you see someone as yourself, compassion follows.

THIS IS ME TRYING

How can you start seeing others as yourself? Maybe if you are quick to judge or comment on someone's mistake, could you instead meet that judgment with curiosity? Alternatively, are there ways you can foster that sense of humanity near you? Instead of going to a box store, maybe try a local small business first. Or maybe you can use your platform to share someone else's work. Overtime, these small questions and actions will help you see others more as yourself.

MEDITATION 3

There Is Good in the World

Today's chaotic and often cruel world can feel really heavy, unfair, and even dangerous. For someone like Taylor, that terror or danger can feel especially heightened. She has been stalked, sexually assaulted, and even had to cancel three The Eras Tour shows in Vienna because of an ISIS terrorist threat that was very real.

Reflecting on some of these feelings in an *Elle* magazine essay, she said, "There was a tremendous amount of planning, expense, and effort put into keeping my fans safe. My fear of violence has continued into my personal life. I carry QuikClot army-grade bandage dressing, which is for gunshot or stab wounds. Websites and tabloids have taken it upon themselves to post every home address I've ever had online. You get enough stalkers trying to break into your house and you kind of start prepping for bad things."

THIS IS ME TRYING

Take some time to reflect on goodness you have seen in the world lately. What memories can you hold on to when life feels chaotic? Keep those reminders close so you can continue to move through life with flow, ease, and compassion.

However, despite all that, she continued to reflect and say, "Every day I try to remind myself of the good in the world, the love I've witnessed, and the faith I have in humanity. We have to live bravely in order to truly feel alive, and that means not being ruled by our greatest fears."

The *Tao* reminds us that with compassion, one is courageous. With the heaviness and brokenness that exist in our world, it's important not to lose sight of our humanity, our humility, and our compassion for one another. Life flows best when we trust, soften, and remain open to the good that is present.

MEDITATION 4

Service Toward Others

In 2012, Kevin McGuire, a cancer survivor, invited Taylor to be his date for prom on a Facebook page. The post amassed thousands of views and even caught the attention of Taylor. She responded by posting on his page and said, "Kevin, I'm so sorry but I won't be able to make it to your prom. But I was wondering, the ACM Awards are coming up . . . Would you be my date? Love, Taylor."

Shortly before the award show, however, Kevin's cancer returned and he was unable to attend. Taylor gave him a shoutout in her award speech and called him on the phone. However, the following year, Taylor made good on her promise, inviting Kevin to the award show now that he was feeling better. Throughout her career, Taylor has always found ways to give back—whether through financial donations or moments like this with fans.

The *Tao* shares that the universe and the Earth are eternal and lasting because they do not simply exist for the betterment of themselves, but for others, and this is why they endure. To be compassionate and kind is to recognize that we are all part of the same whole and no one person is better than another. Being kind is not about faking niceties, it's about recognizing our humanity and understanding what is truly important.

When we put others first, not in a self-sacrifice way, but in one that recognizes our shared wholeness, we discover that true greatness lies in that humility, connection, and care toward one another. Taylor did not bring home any awards the night that she and Kevin attended the ACM Awards. However, the *Tao* reminds us that when you are not focused on outcomes or achievements, you always succeed, and that kindness is the ultimate prize in this life.

THIS IS ME TRYING

What if greatness was not measured by awards, achievements, or accolades, but instead by those quiet ways that you can bring more care and kindness to the world? What are some ways you can quietly bring more kindness into spaces and areas in your own life?

MEDITATION 5

Remember This Moment

The Tao *reminds us that words can make an impact, but it's the kind actions that can change or even save lives. Since the beginning of her career, Taylor has always given back in big ways, like through large-scale donations and staff bonuses, but she has also given back in smaller, kind ways like one-on-one hospital visits and connecting directly with her fans—for whom she constantly expresses her gratitude.*

THIS IS ME TRYING

You don't have to have a lot of money or a large platform like Taylor to make a difference. You can invite someone new to town over for dinner, you can write a letter to someone who played an important role in your life, or you can simply give someone that much-needed hug.

During the rollout for Taylor's *1989* album, she decided to do something almost unheard of in the celebrity realm. She invited eighty-nine fans to each of her five houses (LA, Nashville, New York, Rhode Island, and London), and she gave them the opportunity to be the first to listen to her new record before it was released into the world.

When discussing why she decided to do this, she shared that she wanted to do something where she could meet more of her fans who have been there and supported her all these years and do something really special for them. It started with a simple idea and then with more excitement and ideas, it eventually morphed into what became known as the *1989* Secret Sessions and she went on to do them for *Reputation* and *Lover* as well. For all the sessions, Taylor baked homemade cookies, ordered pizza, and took photos with every single guest, creating an incredible experience that these fans will remember and cherish forever.

Taylor once said, "I'm never the first one to pull away from a hug because I don't know how much that person needs it." While her music is what sells, her kindness is what saves. Kind actions save lives. They help others and they can even help you.

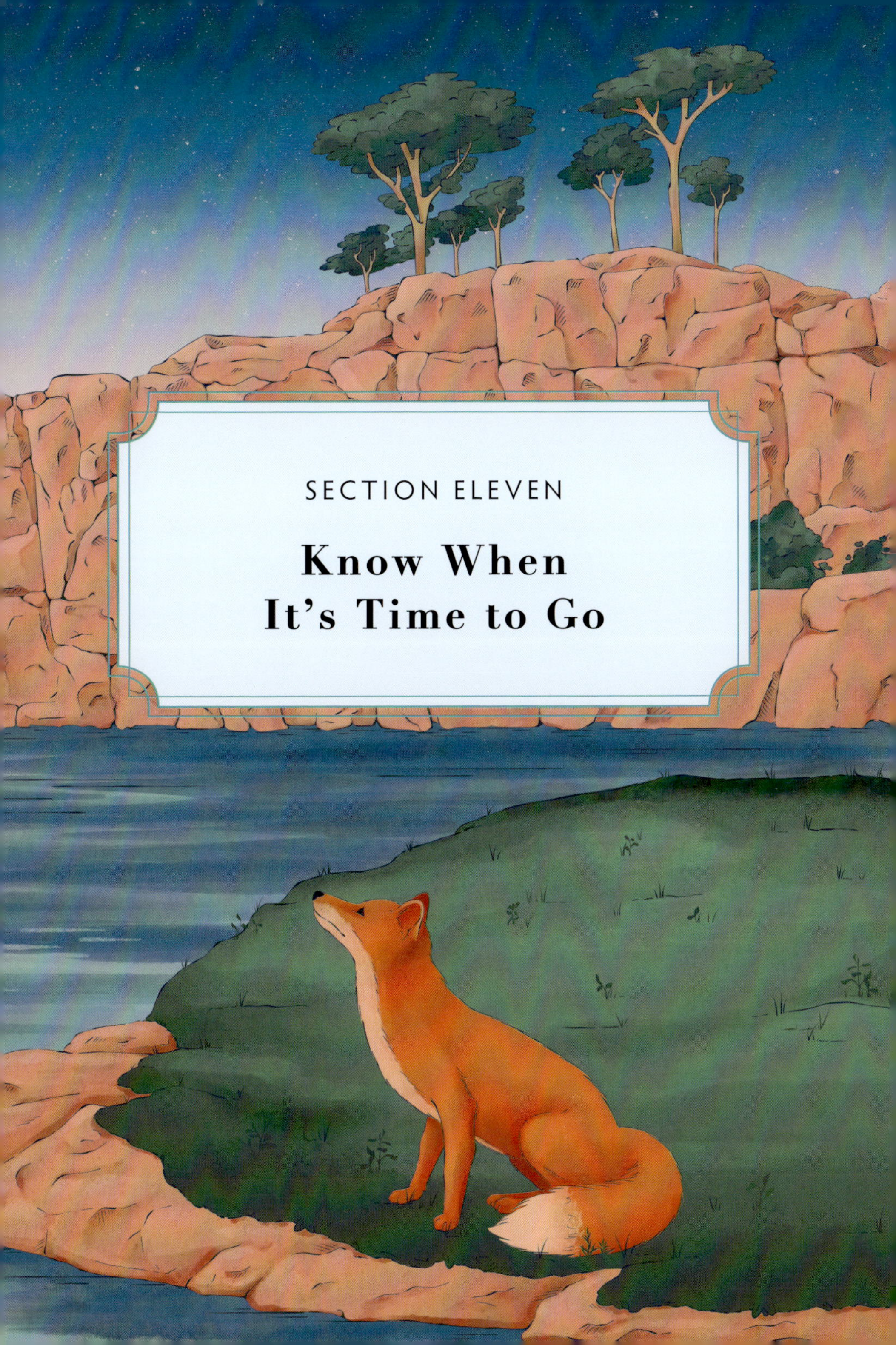

SECTION ELEVEN

Know When It's Time to Go

The rigid and stiff will be broken.

The soft and yielding will overcome.

THE *TAO*, CHAPTER 76

But I think that, you know, if something's toxic and it's only ever really been that, what are you going to do? Just move on. It's fine.

TAYLOR

MEDITATION 1

Turn Off the Comments

In an essay Taylor penned for Elle *magazine, she said, "One thing I do to lessen this weird insecurity laser beam is to turn off comments. Yes, I keep comments off on my posts. That way, I'm showing my friends and fans updates on my life, but I'm training my brain to not need the validation of someone telling me that I look 🔥🔥🔥. I'm also blocking out anyone who might feel the need to tell me to 'go die in a hole ho' while I'm having my coffee at nine in the morning. I think it's healthy for your self-esteem to need less Internet praise to appease it, especially when three comments down you could unwittingly see someone*

THIS IS ME TRYING

When the comments get loud, how can you turn them off? Will you physically turn the comments section off? Or can you find a place to rest when the noise gets too loud? How can you shake off the comments to find your own inner peace?

telling you that you look like a weasel that got hit by a truck and stitched back together by a drunk taxidermist. An actual comment I received once."

The Tao teaches that both praise and criticism can cause alarm. If we find value in what others think of us, whether it's praise and accolades or whether it's negative comments and trolling, we can no longer trust ourselves.

Taylor's proactive approach to turning comments off is a modern act of wu wei (effortless action): removing the external stimulus so she can flow with her life without constantly resisting or seeking validation.

In our social media world where everyone has an opinion, it's easy to only want to read the good comments or fixate on the one negative comment, but Taylor's approach is showing that not fixating on either is a way to keep her centered and continuously moving with the flow of life.

MEDITATION 2

Saying "No" Is a Complete Sentence

At age fourteen, Taylor took her demo CD up and down Music Row in Nashville, TN. She eventually caught the eye of RCA Records and they offered her a developmental deal. This was what so many young artists could only dream of and certainly something Taylor was dreaming about for years. However, once they got into the details of the deal, the folks at RCA wanted Taylor to cover other songs and spend the next year working on her overall development as an artist. Taylor, however, had written hundreds of songs and was ready to release an album sooner than later. To everyone's surprise, she ended up turning down the deal.

A little while later, she was performing at the iconic Bluebird Café in Nashville and caught the attention of a music executive with a new label. After her set, he told Taylor that he was starting a new label and would love to sign her. Taylor took that chance, and shortly later, she released her debut album, *Taylor Swift*.

Stepping away from something or saying "no" can be difficult, especially if your ego is in play. Taylor wasn't saying, "OMG, but it's RCA Records—one of the biggest record labels out there! I should stick it out!" Instead, she was saying, "I created this music and I want to release it sooner rather than later." So she went with a small indie label that wasn't even off the ground yet to do just that.

Following your intuition, or that gut feeling, helps you continue to align with the Way of the Tao. When you can release your ego and tap into your intuition, you are able to drown out the noise and continue to go with the flow of life.

Turning down something seemingly big and life-changing can feel scary. You might think, "Will I ever get another chance like this again?" But if you can see the vision for your goals and that offer doesn't fit, it's okay to say, "No." Taylor shows us that it's okay to wait to find your place in the world and to say "yes" to the things that are a "hell yes!"

THIS IS ME TRYING

What is something you followed your gut instinct on and ending up aligning? Alternatively, what is something that you said "yes" to out of Ego or obligation that you ended up regretting? Ultimately, what did you learn from both that can keep you flowing on your own path?

MEDITATION 3

Persuade with Words, Not Weapons

Going through a break-up? There's a song for that. Feeling extreme loss? There is a song for that. Have a sick parent, friend, or family member? There's a song for that. Ending a business relationship? There's a song for that. Happy and want to dance? There is a song for that. For all life's emotions, there is a Taylor Swift song for that.

THIS IS ME TRYING

Consider how you can put pen to paper and create change around you. Write a letter to your mayor. Send an email to your local representative. Not sure how to get through to someone? Try writing them a letter. There is power in the pen!

Taylor has used songwriting to get her through almost every emotion. Talking about her songwriting, she said, "I've never thought about songwriting as a weapon. I've only thought about it as a way to help me get through love and loss and sadness and loneliness and growing up."

Aside from songwriting, Taylor has used her words when it mattered most. She penned a letter to Apple for better treatment of artists on their platform, to which they responded and immediately changed their policies. When she broke her political silence and put a call out to register to vote, there was a surge of new voters.

Whether it is a catchy melody encouraging you to shake it off or calm down, or a call to action, Taylor persuades with her words. Similarly, the Tao teaches us that great leaders and changemakers don't dominate or control but instead use patience and the power of their words to create change.

MEDITATION 4

Don't Be Afraid to Jump Then Fall

After losing the Grammy Album of the Year award for her album Red, *Taylor allowed herself to feel sad for a little while (with the help of an In-N-Out burger that softened the blow). Then she woke up at four a.m. the next day with the vision for her next album* 1989, *and said, "I'm calling it a pop record and I'm not listening to anyone at my record label. I'm starting tomorrow."*

While the Grammy loss was definitely a catalyst, it helped her turn to her intuition, and she quit overthinking everyone else's opinions on what she should do with her creativity, music, or career. Up until that point, Taylor took cues from those surrounding her, including her family, her team, and the music executives. However, this moment is when we see Taylor fully embrace her intuition and creative pursuits.

Taylor was later asked by Barbara Walters if she worried that she would lose some of her country fans by making the switch. Taylor confidently said, "I am not worried about that. I am really in touch with my fans and I know what they like. What my fans in general were afraid of is that I would start making pop music and I would stop writing smart lyrics or I would stop writing emotional lyrics. And when they heard the new music, they realized that that wasn't the case at all."

The Tao reminds us to tap into our inner knowing and to continue to move to our own natural timing. If you are worried about what everyone else thinks before creating something, it can lead to both internal and external resistance, or even worse, abandoning the creation all together. However, like Taylor and the Tao teach us, when you deeply know yourself and trust yourself, you can make decisions that feel easeful to you, and you will naturally allow the current to take you to the next step. The outcome is not what matters, but it's about enjoying the ride on the way there.

THIS IS ME TRYING

If you are feeling a shift or change in your career or life, listen to your gut. Maybe you write nonfiction books and want to try writing fiction. Try it! Maybe you've spent your entire career in the nonprofit world, but really want to open a bakery. Go for it! You never know if you don't try, and you might be surprised where the currents could take you next, especially when you let go of the resistance and just let it flow naturally.

MEDITATION 5

Catch and Release

"Part of growing up and moving into new chapters of your life is about catch and release. What I mean by that is, knowing what things to keep and what things to release. You can't carry all things, all grudges, all updates on your ex, all enviable promotions your school bully got at the hedge fund his uncle started. Decide what is yours to hold and let the rest go. Oftentimes the good things in your life are lighter anyway, so there's more room for them. One toxic relationship can outweigh so many wonderful, simple joys. You get to pick what your life has time and room for. Be discerning."

THIS IS ME TRYING

In a game of cat and mouse—or catch and release—how can you start releasing more than what you catch? What are you carrying that feels heavy, and what might open up if you allow it to release?

Just like Taylor's wisdom at left, the Tao also aligns with this philosophy—reminding us that letting go can help make space for the things you really want. The *Tao* teaches us that true mastery comes from letting things go their own way and not trying to interfere or hold on so tightly. Wholeness comes not from holding on or trying to accumulate the most knowledge to make the best decision, but rather being discerning and letting go so you can move through life with light and ease.

The "catch and release" Taylor discusses also echoes the *Tao*. We are not meant to carry every burden, grudge, or fear or ghosts from the past. Instead, the Tao encourages us to let go and to make a blank space for joy and peace.

SKS
AS
TS

SECTION TWELVE

It's None of My Business

It is better not to speak of things you do not understand.

THE TAO, CHAPTER 5

My name can be in the actual headline, and it's none of my business.

TAYLOR

Gossip and rumors thrive on judgment and often deeply divide people. The Tao, however, doesn't judge, label, or pick sides. Instead, it understands that every person is a part of the bigger whole and by letting go of judgments or preconceived rumors, you can maintain your energy and compassion, rather than harvesting hatred. And when it comes to rumors or gossip in your own life, the Tao encourages us to continue to walk our own path, staying true to ourselves and quieting the outside noises.

For Taylor, her entire young adult and adult life has been dissected, discussed, and judged—by everyone from random strangers on the Internet to TV hosts to other celebrities. Even presidents have had things to say about her. Taylor has experienced this and more when it comes to being in the public eye. And while this kind of scrutiny used to get to her, she said that she has done things to protect her peace over the years. For example, she doesn't Google herself, she turns comments off on her Instagram posts, and in general, she shields herself from a lot of the outside noise. Instead, she stays in her own lane.

When it comes to relationships with others, the Tao also encourages us to be kind both to the kind and the unkind. During the premier of *Taylor Swift: The Official Release Party of a Showgirl* at AMC Theaters, she discussed sentiment when she talked about the meaning behind her song, "CANCELLED." She said, "I definitely judge people a lot less now that I've been kind of under the microscope for so long." She continues, "I just judge people based on who I know them to be, their actions, not some sort of general consensus where people are like, 'Stay away, they're radioactive.'"

While the Tao encourages kindness to all, it doesn't mean that if someone does something harmful that we tolerate it. It means that you still remain unwavering in your own inner kindness and belief in humanity despite what others do. You can simply wish them well and move along in your own life.

Whether it's a rumor about you or someone else, those outside noises are none of your business. Both Taylor and the Tao remind us that if you stay true to your own knowing and integrity, the outside noises and rumors will quiet and instead, you can allow your energy to flow inward rather than into other people's business.

MEDITATION 1

An Open Heart

In the TIME *2023 Person of the Year article, Taylor talked about how being "cancelled" took her to the lowest place of her life psychologically. She had a hard time trusting people and wondered if that negatively was going to impact her for the rest of her life.*

In 2025, she released her new album, *The Life of a Showgirl.* She shared insight into each of her songs and discussed how the song, "CANCELLED!" was written more as a reflection on empathy and resilience and how those public moments of intense criticism can lead to better understanding and wisdom. She shares, "I kind of wanted to write a song about how you could become wiser for it. You can become sharper, stronger, and maybe even a little kinder."

THIS IS ME TRYING

Have you ever been subject to gossip or negative comments? How have you become wiser, stronger, or more understanding because of it? Alternatively, have you been quick to talk shit with your friends, or gossip about situations you don't know much about? Can you instead find relation and humility rather than judgment?

The Tao teaches that everything transforms into its opposite. Public criticism or "canceling," loss, heartbreak, humiliation—all of these can seem like setbacks, but they can also teach us that every loss is a step we take and those steps can blossom into insight, humility, and better understanding for one another.

In the documentary film *Miss Americana*, Taylor says, "I want to still have a sharp pen and a thin skin and an open heart." This sentiment showcases that no matter what she is going through, no matter how chaotic her world can get or feel, she still wants to remain open to the world around her. Both Taylor's reflections and her song *is* the Tao in motion.

MEDITATION 2

Soon You'll Get Better

Taylor and her mom, Andrea, have always been super close, Taylor calling her mom her "best friend." She recognized how much her mom had been taking care of their family and managing and wanted to make sure her mom was taking care of herself. So, in 2015, Taylor asked her mom to get a full health exam as a precaution. When Andrea finally went to get a checkup, she was unexpectedly diagnosed with cancer. She initially went into remission after treatment, but her cancer came back in 2019. Although the family has been quiet about it, this is unfortunately a universal reality for so many.

Taylor told *Variety* magazine, "It's taught me that there are real problems and then there's everything else. My mom's cancer is a real problem. I used to be so anxious about daily ups and downs. I give all of my worry, stress, and prayers to real problems now."

Like Taylor's own understanding, the Tao also teaches us not to waste our energy on the small stuff and instead remain rooted in what's important. The Tao also reminds us that caution and courage must be balanced. An illness or diagnosis, both for the person and the family, reflects this delicate balance. Caution teaches us to rest, listen, and adapt. Courage calls us to face what lies ahead and to move forward, even if it feels uncertain or difficult. Too much caution becomes fear, and too much courage can result in toxic positivity and burnout. It's not about never feeling either of those emotions, but instead, recognizing that both are a part of the journey.

THIS IS ME TRYING

It's easy to get caught up in the day-to-day stressors of life. When you do ask yourself, "Is this a real problem?" oftentimes it's not. How can you instead put your energy into those things that require care and truly matter?

MEDITATION 3

Karma

Karma has become synonymous with Taylor Swift. She talks about it in interviews and even released a song called "Karma" on the Midnights *album. In a 2016* Vogue *"73 Questions" interview, Taylor is asked what the most important lesson for someone to learn is, and she responds, "That karma's real."*

In *Reputation*, we hear Taylor talk about "karma" in the most common sense that karma will come to get you, shedding light on the fact that if you do someone wrong, you will get what you deserve in this life. The album itself carries a "revenge" vibe. Then in *Midnights*, Taylor turns karma around and showcases how she experiences karma, signaling all the good things in her life like her cats and her relaxing thoughts, almost as a reward for her "good" karma. In both cases, we see karma used more as a punishment and reward system.

THIS IS ME TRYING

While revenge and the traditional sense of someone "getting their karma" can feel good in the moment, they are temporary thrills and not sustainable long-term. Instead, rather than hoping karma will "get" someone, can you take the approach of indifference? Can you wish your protagonist well and move along, trusting that it will eventually balance out. Admittedly it's not much of a thrill, but it is ultimately what will give you peace.

However, in Taoism, karma is not about a punishment and reward system, but instead, it's about allowing the natural order of the world to balance itself, and if we keep moving along, it will balance out. There is no action you need to take and no fixation on when it will happen.

On *The Tortured Poets Department* album (anthology edition), we see this growth from the reward/punishment style of "karma" to a more Taoist approach in the song "thanK you aIMee." The song is allegedly about her ongoing feud with Kim Kardashian, noting in the song that even though someone is bullying her, she is going to just continue with her life and let it balance out. Then toward the end of the song, she even acknowledges that without this person and this experience, no matter how bad it was, she wouldn't have been led to where she is now, essentially thanking her protagonist and showing that it eventually did work out.

MEDITATION 4

Mirrorball

Taylor's song "mirrorball" describes someone yearning to be seen, like a disco ball hanging and twinkling in the nighttime light. This song describes this person getting on their highest tiptoes and willing to change everything about them to fit in.

When discussing the song, Taylor says it was a metaphor for celebrity, but also a metaphor for anyone who feels like they have to change for other people or be different versions of themselves around others—like at work or school or around certain groups of friends.

She said this is the first song she wrote specifically about the lockdown experience, saying, "I wrote this song right after all my shows were canceled." She continues, "I realized here I am writing all this music, still trying. And I know I have an excuse to sit back and not do something, but I'm not and I don't know why that is."

She took an introspective approach, using this song as the metaphor, wondering why she couldn't just sit back and do nothing. However, creating and being in motion is the way of the universe, so it makes sense that she wanted to keep creating art. However, I think she was really asking herself those bigger questions, like "Am I writing these songs to continue to display myself and for the applause?" or "Am I doing this because creation keeps me in the flow?"

The Tao, however, reminds us that staying grounded is what keeps you in the flow. The *Tao* says that you will not find true happiness or growth on a display or pedestal or shining in front of a crowd, but rather once you are grounded in who you are. Through the song and the commentary, we see Taylor confront this issue of creation versus Ego, wrestling with her own desires to be seen versus her desire to be in motion and creating.

THIS IS ME TRYING

The Tao reminds us of this constant delicate balance and encourages us to remain grounded, so we don't lose balance in who we are. Are you seeking validation by standing on tiptoe, or are you rooted in who you are, trusting that true growth and joy come from staying grounded? What are ways you can ensure you stay rooted in who you are, especially when your Ego starts becoming louder?

MEDITATION 5

One of These Things Is Not Like the Other

During the launch of her album Midnights, *Taylor went on* The Tonight Show Starring Jimmy Fallon *to share all about her upcoming record. During the interview she said, "I'm feeling very overwhelmed by the fans' love for the record. I'm also feeling, like, very soft and fragile, so the two can exist at once."*

THIS IS ME TRYING

The next time you are in between two conflicting feelings, stop and allow yourself space to hold them both. What can each feeling teach you about the present moment of where you are?

This quote immediately stood out because it's rare to hear someone so candidly share the dualities so many of us experience. We can feel the excitement of something new we put into the world, while also feeling scared about it no longer being only ours. We can feel both overwhelmed and grateful. Strong and soft. Fulfilled and fragile. These are not contradictions, but instead complements of each other.

The Tao reminds us that opposites—like difficulty and ease, loud and soft, and high and low—seem contradictory, but they are revealed in one another. Two feelings can be present, and we don't have to choose one over the other, but we can instead sit with both. It's important to not get caught in either feeling with rigidness but to instead feel those feelings and let them continue to flow through you. In a world that seems to be constantly run by black-and-white thinking, the Tao is a beautiful reminder of the nuance and the space in between.

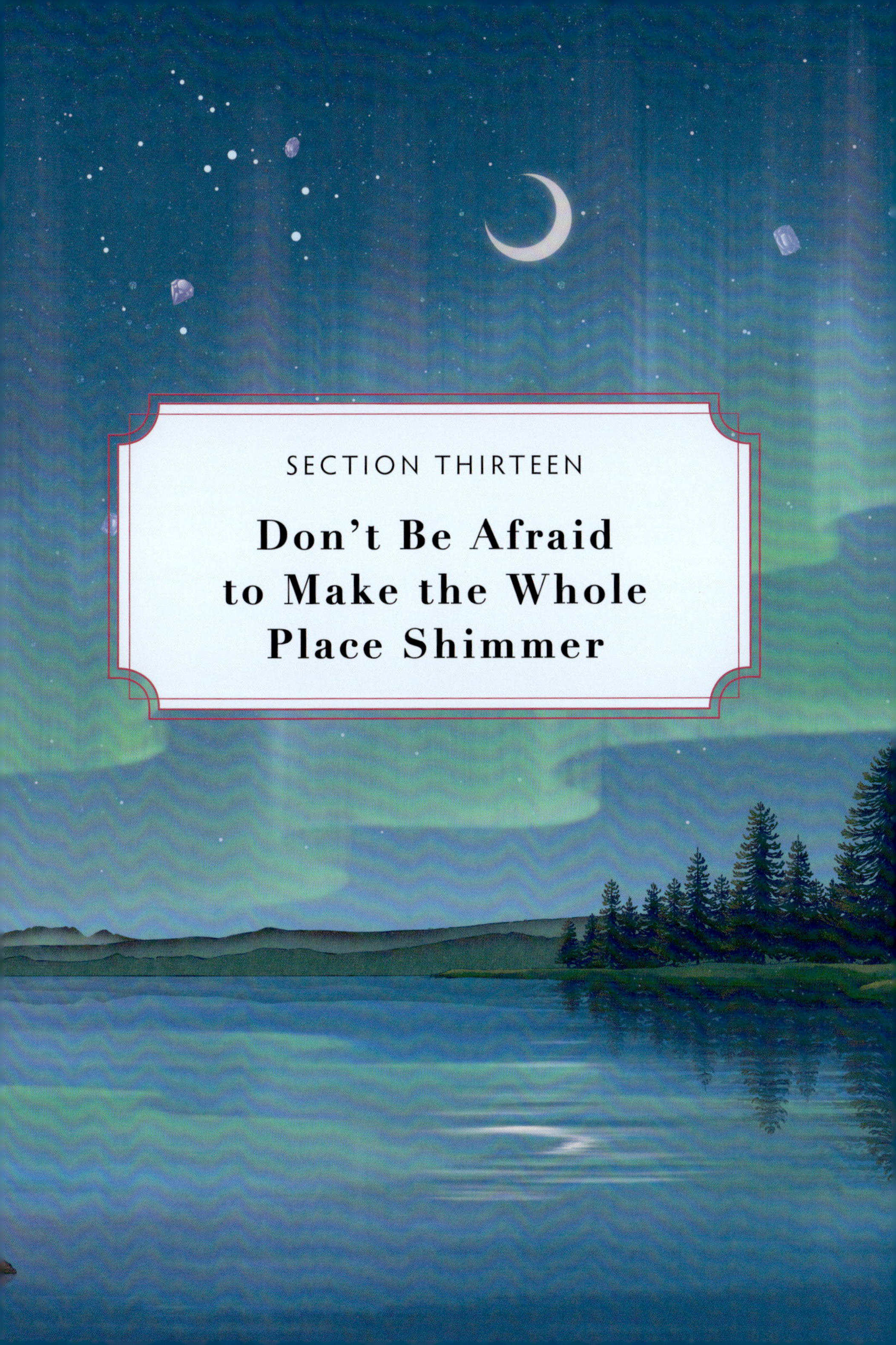

SECTION THIRTEEN

Don't Be Afraid to Make the Whole Place Shimmer

To grow, yet not to control: This is the mysterious virtue.

THE *TAO*, CHAPTER 10

I've found that growing up can mean a lot of things. For me, it doesn't mean I should become somebody completely new and stop loving the things I used to love. It means I've just added more things to my list.

TAYLOR

The Tao reminds us that having a childlike mentality or wonder can move us with more ease throughout the world. The Tao *says, "One who is filled with the Tao is like a newborn child. The infant is protected from the stinging insects, wild beasts, and birds of prey. Its bones are soft, its muscles are weak, but its grip is firm and strong," reminding us that children don't know anything about the power structures of the world, but they have a life force within them that is unshakable.*

As we age, we forget that joy, curiosity, and play are a part of us, and we can often let the world weigh us down. Excitement, joy, and play are all contagious, and if we allow that force to stay within us, our light will never dim and we can move through life with more ease along the way.

When Taylor walks in the room, she makes the whole place shimmer and not just because of her sparkly sequin outfits, but because she is one of the most excitable people on the planet—a constant cheerleader to those around her. She's the first to acknowledge and cheer on her team, her friends and family, and always makes sure to shoutout people she admires. From winning an award to performing in front of a crowd of any size, Taylor always brings a sense of wide-eyed amazement and genuine excitement. For someone that has won so many awards and performed on the biggest stages, you would think that excitement would diminish, but it hasn't. She maintains her childlike wonder and awe.

Just like the Tao and Taylor, we don't have to force our own light to shine. When we move forward in our own unique paths, it shimmers alongside us and gives us the energy to keep going.

MEDITATION 1

Tour Pranks

Before headlining her own tours, Taylor opened for major country acts such as Rascal Flatts and Keith Urban. In 2009, Taylor opened for Keith's Escape Together World Tour and, at the time, his song "Kiss A Girl" was a big hit.

While the tour was getting close to wrapping up, there was a tour tradition of pranking each other and Taylor brought her best prank yet. During the song "Kiss A Girl," Taylor and her band crashed the set dressed as members of KISS. An unrecognizable Taylor dressed as Ace Frehley ended up performing the hit song alongside Keith, who was shocked and amused, laughing as he stepped aside to let Taylor sing part of the chorus.

THIS IS ME TRYING

By approaching the world with lightness, humor, and creativity, we allow joy to flow alongside purpose. Rigid seriousness can blind us to the spontaneous, delightful moments that make life fun. How can you bring more play to your life?

Then during The Red Tour, her opener Ed Sheeran did something similar. He dressed up as a joker and launched on stage during the set, shocking and confusing Taylor and then filling her with laughter and joy.

Moments like these remind us to engage in the world lightly, to have fun, laugh, and move creatively and playfully without rigidness or attachment. The Tao reminds us that you can be full of meaning and depth while still being playful. If we were serious all the time, we would not know playfulness, and like the Tao teaches us, both coexist together.

MEDITATION 2

We All Have Crowns

The media loves to pit women against each other, and we've seen this time and time again with Taylor and other pop stars. From award-show drama to tabloids and to dissecting every single caption or album rollout—there always seems to be something the media or the Internet fixates on to pit two people against each other.

Taylor addressed this issue in her music video, "You Need to Calm Down." In the video, there is a scene set up to mimic a beauty pageant, featuring several drag queens dressed up as famous pop stars who are competing against each other. The pop stars include Katy Perry, Ariana Grande, Cardi B, Beyoncé, Adele, Lady Gaga, Nicki Minaj, and of course, Taylor. RuPaul comes out carrying a crown to award the winner, but he instead tosses it in the air, and the song anthem plays, reminding them that they all have crowns, before the scene erupts into an epic food fight. It's a fun scene full of laughter and play, while recognizing that no one pop star is better than another, but in fact, everyone is amazing exactly as they are.

To recognize the value in all things is to live in harmony with the Tao. Just like in nature—from the smallest insect to a vast river—everything has a role and purpose, or like Taylor reminds us, we all have crowns. So why spend time pitting everyone against each other when everyone is killing it in their own way? The Tao doesn't play favorites, and neither should you.

THIS IS ME TRYING

How can you embrace the idea that we all have crowns? If you find yourself comparing yourself to someone's shiny Internet reel, can you instead take a moment to celebrate them and celebrate yourself as well?

MEDITATION 3

Let Your Style Be Ever-Changing

In 2022, Taylor received an honorary doctorate degree from New York University. During her commencement speech, she talked about her style and fashion, saying, "I promise you, you're probably doing or wearing something right now that you will look back on later and find revolting and hilarious. You can't avoid it, so don't try to. For example, I had a phase where, for the entirety of 2012, I dressed like a 1950s housewife. But you know what? I was having fun. Trends and phases are fun. Looking back and laughing is fun."

THIS IS ME TRYING

Just like your style, how can you allow yourself to embrace change? What would you do, wear, or create if you stopped worrying about whether it seemed "cringe" and just let it flow?

Taylor also once said, "I would describe my own style as something that is sort of ever-changing." While she is talking about style and fashion in these quotes, she's also metaphorically talking about embracing your uniqueness throughout your life. Having a playful spirit about something as simple as fashion can help us carry that same playful energy throughout life. At one point those fashion choices brought joy, and years later they might bring a little cringe, one that you can hopefully laugh at, which in turn, can also bring you joy.

Similarly, the Tao teaches us that it's okay to change direction and let go of things from the past. The Tao reminds us that we contain multitudes, and whether it's short skirts or T-shirts, or Louboutins or Keds, we can draw on different energies and styles at different times in our life. After all, to live in balance with the Tao is to embrace your ever-changing self.

MEDITATION 4

Be Your Own Cheerleader

She might not have been a cheer captain, but Taylor has an infectious excitement for life. She spreads this excitement when she shares a new album or music video. Or when she discusses her enthusiasm for sourdough bread. Or when she's cheering on her future husband's football team. She is a big advocate for enthusiasm and she shares about it in her NYU commencement speech, saying, "I'm a big advocate for not hiding your enthusiasm for things. It seems to me that there is a false stigma around eagerness in our culture of 'unbothered ambivalence.' This outlook perpetuates the idea that it's not cool to 'want it.'

That people who don't try hard are fundamentally more chic than people who do. And I wouldn't know because I have been a lot of things but I've never been an expert on 'chic.'"

When we share our excitement with the world, we might be met with resistance. We might be told to dim our light, silence our excitement, or dull our sparkle to try to fit in or to seem unbothered. But the Tao reminds us that the flow of the universe isn't one way. Rivers rush, trees bloom, flowers burst with dazzling colors. Just like in nature, excitement is a natural part of life and a beautiful part of our world. To dim your enthusiasm would be to resist your own nature.

THIS IS ME TRYING

How can you let your excitement ripple out without trying to resist or contain it? Allow yourself to feel those excited feelings for both yourself and others. Instead of bypassing an award or birthday, give yourself permission to celebrate it. Excitement is a sign of that energy moving freely—proof you are alive, present, and connected to the flow.

MEDITATION 5

Dance on Your Own

She might not be a natural dancer, but she tries, tries, tries—and her energy is contagious. At award shows, Taylor can often be seen as the only one in the room standing and dancing to her fellow performers. During a 1989 listening session, she discusses these award-show moments and how she has the best time dancing to the coolest artists, but everyone else seems bored by it.

She says, "Those are the greatest artists out right now and they're performing for you. I just decided I would have fun with it so I'm always, like, up and dancing and I'm really tall and lanky so I look a little bit like a baby giraffe learning how to walk. But all over the Internet it would be like, 'Taylor looks awkward when she dances. She's so bad at dancing!' And so the way I handle that now, that criticism. I wrote a song called

THIS IS ME TRYING

Has there been a time where you like others criticism or words dull something you genuinely enjoy? How can or would you handle it next time so that you can still experience joy in the things you love?

'Shake It Off,' and as soon as I wrote the song I knew exactly what I wanted to do for the music video. I knew that I wanted to do an entire music video of me awkwardly, badly dancing."

She continues, "If you learn to laugh at certain things and not take everything so seriously. If something hurts your feelings that's valid and you're allowed to let that happen, but I'm just kind of like, yeah, I do dance awkwardly and I'm having more fun than you."

The Tao reminds us that if we treat things like social rules, status, and money so seriously, we will never be satisfied. The Tao encourages returning to childlike lightness—allowing yourself to celebrate, play, and to remember what awe feels like. Taylor shook off the criticism, literally and figuratively by choosing to dance and feel that joy that comes along with not taking yourself too seriously. Whether you're dancing in the middle of a parking lot, in your PJ's before school, or in the middle of the room when the night ends, continue to dance to the beat of your own drum, whatever that means for you.

MEDITATION 6

Perfectionism Isn't the Goal

When we place others, like Taylor, on pedestals, we forget that they are also flowing along the same messy, windy, crooked path of life that we are, too. And when we try to define or find that "perfectionism," we will naturally be disappointed as the way of life is not one of rigidness. The Tao invites us to step outside of our dualistic thinking and instead, see others (and ourselves) as both whole and messy, constantly evolving parts of one balance.

During the *1989* tour, Taylor shared a nightly speech before she performed her song, "Clean." During the Chicago stop she shared, "I don't think any of us can aspire to have some kind of perfect life. I think we can aspire to continue to keep going when our life doesn't feel perfect." And she continued on this sentiment at the Tokyo stop saying, "When you have bad days that just won't let up, I just hope that you will look in the mirror and remind yourself of what you are, and what you are not. You are not your mistakes. You are not damaged goods or money from your failed explorations. You are not the opinion of someone who doesn't know you. You are a product of the lessons you have learned. You are wiser because you went through something terrible. And you are the person who survived a bunch of rainstorms and kept walking. I now believe that pain makes you stronger. I now believe that walking through a lot of rainstorms gets you clean."

THIS IS ME TRYING

Expecting perfection in our own life or the life of our favorite pop star is unrealistic and it only sets us up for failure. Instead, how can we love someone's light (or your own) without denying their shadow? That is harmony. That is the Way of the Tao. And that is what will ultimately keep you flowing.

Conclusion

This Is Not the End of All the Endings

When Taylor was twenty-four, an interviewer asked her where she thought she would be in ten years. Taylor responded, "I'd really like to let life happen rather than have some weird plan for it. I think if you have a plan for like 'I need to be married by this age' and 'I need to have kids by this age' you'll kind of force your life to take that course and you might not end up with the right person, you might be making decisions under duress of your own plans and I just want to let my life happen."

Time, curious time—that's the mystery and the beauty of the Tao so perfectly displayed in Taylor's quote. The Tao reminds us that nature doesn't need to hurry, resist, or control, and yet, everything is accomplished. With no compasses or signs, if we loosen the grip, we can let life take us right where we were meant to be. And if we remain gentle with ourselves and bend throughout the many currents of life, we can find both "peace" and "happiness" along the way. We just have to continue to let life happen.

ACKNOWLEDGMENTS

The *Tao Te Ching* by Lao-Tzu—This book would not exist without the wisdom from Lao-Tzu's *Tao Te Ching*. I am forever grateful to my early introduction to this work and the many translators who brought this text to the masses.

Taylor Swift—Your words, your music, your resilience, and your ability to keep going with the flow through every season is awe-inspiring and has changed my life in so many ways.

Dr. Ted Cibik—As a teenager, you were able to get through to me and your impact has rippled throughout my life and career. Thank you for changing my life for the better.

Eva Scalzo—Not only are you my ride or die Swiftie and favorite concert partner, but you championed this book to the finish line and I am forever grateful.

Karyn Gerhard—I have seen you transform to a Swiftie right before my eyes! Thank you so much for your editorial guidance and elevating this book in ways beyond my wildest dreams.

Megan Sinead Bingham—Your creative direction and love of the fandom truly made this book the most gorgeous book it could be. Thank you for making it shine.

Laurie-Anne Poquet—Your illustrations truly make this book dazzling. Thank you for helping my words come to life with your art.

Swifties—I'm so thankful for all the magic we made throughout the years whether it was in an online space or at a live show. Long live!

ABOUT THE AUTHOR

Lindsey Smith is a publishing professional and the author of several books, including two other Taylor Swift–inspired books, Bake It Off *and* Taylor Swift Chronicles. *Her personal work has appeared in* PopSugar; Cosmopolitan; Parade *magazine; the* Chicago Tribune; *ABC; NBC; CBS, and her parents' junk drawer. She recently opened a bookstore, One Idea Books and Gifts, in her hometown of Leechburg, Pennsylvania. She's an OG Swiftie and even worked at Taylor's perfume booth during The Red Tour. To learn more about Lindsey, visit www.TheLindseySmith.com.*

weldon**owen**
an imprint of Insight Editions
P.O. Box 3088
San Rafael, CA 94912
www.weldonowen.com

For complete references and additional resources, scan this QR code:

CEO Raoul Goff
SVP Group Publisher Jeff McLaughlin
VP Publisher Roger Shaw
Associate Publisher Thom O'Hearn
Executive Editor Karyn Gerhard
Editorial Assistant Jon Ellis
Production Editor Ivy Long
Art Director & Designer Megan Sinead Bingham
Production Designer Jean Hwang
VP Manufacturing Alix Nicholaeff
Senior Production Manager Greg Steffen
Strategic Production Planner Lina s Palma-Temena

Art by Laurie-Anne Poquet

Weldon Owen would also like to thank Ellen Foreman and Joanne Farness.

Tao text excerpted from *Tao Te Ching - Written by Lao-Tzu: A Translation for the Public Domain* by J. H. McDonald, 1996.

ISBN: 979-8-88674-328-9

Manufactured in China by Insight Editions
10 9 8 7 6 5 4 3 2 1

ROOTS of PEACE REPLANTED PAPER